The Philosophical Novel as a Literary Genre

Michael H. Mitias

The Philosophical Novel as a Literary Genre

palgrave
macmillan

Michael H. Mitias
Department of Philosophy
Millsaps College
Jackson, TN, USA

ISBN 978-3-030-97384-1   ISBN 978-3-030-97385-8 (eBook)
https://doi.org/10.1007/978-3-030-97385-8

© The Editor(s) (if applicable) and The Author(s), under exclusive licence to Springer Nature Switzerland AG 2022
This work is subject to copyright. All rights are solely and exclusively licensed by the Publisher, whether the whole or part of the material is concerned, specifically the rights of translation, reprinting, reuse of illustrations, recitation, broadcasting, reproduction on microfilms or in any other physical way, and transmission or information storage and retrieval, electronic adaptation, computer software, or by similar or dissimilar methodology now known or hereafter developed.
The use of general descriptive names, registered names, trademarks, service marks, etc. in this publication does not imply, even in the absence of a specific statement, that such names are exempt from the relevant protective laws and regulations and therefore free for general use.
The publisher, the authors and the editors are safe to assume that the advice and information in this book are believed to be true and accurate at the date of publication. Neither the publisher nor the authors or the editors give a warranty, expressed or implied, with respect to the material contained herein or for any errors or omissions that may have been made. The publisher remains neutral with regard to jurisdictional claims in published maps and institutional affiliations.

This Palgrave Macmillan imprint is published by the registered company Springer Nature Switzerland AG.
The registered company address is: Gewerbestrasse 11, 6330 Cham, Switzerland

Contents

1 Introduction — 1

2 Basis of Genre in the Literary Novel — 9

3 The Philosophical Novel as a Literary Genre — 45

4 How the Philosophical Novel Communicates Knowledge — 69

5 Analysis of Two Metaphors — 99

6 The Question of Truth in the Philosophical Novel — 119

References and Suggested Bibliography — 139

Index — 143

CHAPTER 1

Introduction

THESIS OF THE BOOK

Whether by creative vision, design, or literary exigency, philosophical themes have been streaming into the literary novel at a fast pace during the past two centuries. Most, if not all, aestheticians and literary theorists refer to these novels as *philosophical* on a par with the generally recognized literary genres such as romantic, mystery, historical, adventure, or religious literary genres in the sphere of the literary novel. Moreover, philosophers use novels such as Tolstoy's *The Death of Ivan Ilych,* Melville's *Moby Dick,* or Camus's *The Myth of Sisyphus* as sources of genuine philosophical knowledge or understanding. Furthermore, during the past seven decades philosophers as well as literary novelists have been writing philosophical novels, as if the boundary between philosophy and literature is transparent, as if the *cognitive ground* on which the philosopher and the literary novelist stand is one and the same, for, how can a novel be philosophical if its theme cannot be expressed, or communicated, in a literary form? How can a philosophy professor discuss a philosophical theme in a literary novel if the theme is not genuinely philosophical? But the relation between philosophy and literature is more intimate than it seems, because as some aestheticians have argued, art can be a philosophy (Kuczynska, "Art as a Philosophy," 2018). If both the philosopher and literary novelist stand on the same cognitive ground, as I shall argue, it would be reasonable to say that the work of a novelist can, at least in principle, be a philosophy. Does the work of the novelist not reflect her worldview (*weltanschauung*)? Is such a view not the spring from which the artist derive her fundamental intuition and interpretation of the values that steer the course of human life at the individual and social levels?

It is not my intention here to explore the relation between philosophy and literature. I made the preceding remark only to emphasize that the relation between them is more intimate than many philosophers and literary theorists tend to think. The possibility of the philosophical novel as a genre, which will occupy my attention throughout this book, is, I think, a vivid indication of this relation. Indeed, we cannot even speak of this possibility if we do not in some way assume that the philosopher and the literary novelist stand on the same cognitive ground.

But although they stand on the same cognitive ground, they are generically different as types of symbolic expression and communication. The way the literary novelist communicates her understanding of one or more aspects of certain values or an aspect of reality is different from the way the philosopher communicates it. Accordingly, when we say, as I shall discuss in some detail, that a literary novel can be philosophical, that a philosopher can be a literary novelist, or that a literary novel can be philosophical, we need to explain how this kind of possibility is viable mainly because the means of literary and philosophical expression and communication are different from each other. The philosopher thinks, argues, demonstrates, and articulates her cognitive intuition conceptually, propositionally. Establishing the truth of her knowledge is one of her central aims as a philosopher. Can the literary novelist argue or establish the truth of the knowledge she communicates? Again, the datum of philosophical thinking is concept; the datum of the literary novelist is image. The philosopher thinks; the literary novelist depicts. How can philosophical knowledge be communicated in the medium of depiction or image? Alas! Can the novelist depict a philosophical concept in the fullness of its meaning and truth? Can she depict a thread of reasoning? For example, although in a romantic novel romance thrives in the hearts of the characters, it can be depicted because its means of communication is to a large extent behavioral: holding hands, kissing, blushing, walking in the garden, stealing glances, embracing, touching, sharing experiences. These gestures and activities come to life when they are accompanied by poetic or romantic expressions such as "I missed you deeply," "I love you madly," or "I worship at the altar of your beauty!" Such expressions objectify the romantic presence that pulsates in the hearts of the lovers!

But philosophical activity is not only subjective, but also *abstract* and cannot be objectified behaviorally. The novelist can, like Rodin in *The Thinker*, portray a philosopher in the mode of deep reflection, but she cannot depict the content of the thinker's reflection, and I doubt that she can depict the content of her own reflection. Is it an accident that this sculpture is titled the "The Thinker" and not "The Poet," "The Novelist," "The Scientist," or "The Philosopher"? The novel may contain one or several philosophical discourses, but, as I shall argue, the mere presence of such discourses does not make the novel philosophical. Thus, if the literary novelist can communicate philosophical knowledge, and she can, it is critically important that she, or the aesthetician, provide an explanation of the kind of magic she uses in transforming the logical and conceptual content of philosophical thinking into a depictive form of symbolic expression. Deciphering the secret of this magic is a necessary condition for classifying philosophical novel as a genre. We may speak of "philosophical novel" honorifically, but can we use this expression in a literary, veritable, or bona fide sense? The claim that this magic is possible underlies the argument of this book, namely, literary novel can communicate philosophical knowledge or understanding; consequently, it should be classified as a genre on a par with the generally recognized genres within the sphere of the literary novel.

In what follows I shall, first, clarify and define some of the basic concepts that are essential to the development of the argument I advance in support of the thesis that the philosophical novel is a literary genre on a par with the generally recognized literary genres such as adventure, mystery, romantic, or religious genres. I emphasize this point at the outset primarily to assure the reader that my discussion of the thesis is not subjective or personal; on the contrary, it is supported by a rigorous line of reasoning. Second, I shall present an outline of the argument I plan to use in support of my thesis. This argument will include seven main propositions. I shall elucidate and defend the validity of each proposition. The purpose of this argument is to show as clearly as possible that, first, the various parts of the book are logically required for an adequate defense of the thesis, second, a literary novel can communicate philosophical knowledge, and, third, metaphor is the vehicle of communicating his type of knowledge. If we assert that the philosophical novel is a literary genre, it should follow that it is cognitive; and if it is cognitive, we should be able to explain how it is communicated. This logical demand underlies the analysis of metaphor as a figure of speech in Chaps. 5 and 6.

Some Basic Concepts

First, literariness. The word "literariness" is derived from the word "literary," which is derived from "literature." As I shall explain in the second and third chapters, although the literary novel is a story, not every story is a literary novel. We should, accordingly, ask, what makes a novel a *literary* work? The focus of this question is in on "literary": What justifies characterizing a novel as a literary work? Or what is the defining feature of literature? The proposition I shall defend is that the literary dimension of the literary novel is the same dimension that makes it a work of art. This dimension consists of the unity of the aesthetic qualities that inhere as a potentiality in the formal organization of the work. The presence of these qualities in any artifact makes it art. When I characterize an artifact as art, I mean it is a work of art. Thus, as a concept, "literariness" refers to the literary, or artistic dimension, of any work in the area of literature regardless of whether it is poetry, novel, short story, elegy, epic, or play. We can add that literariness refers to a basic stratum of the literary work of art (see Ingarden 1973).

Second, philosophicalness. The word "philosophicalness" is derived from the word "philosophical," which is in turn derived from the word "philosophy." "Philosophicalness" refers to those features that define philosophy as an activity, as a method of inquiry, as a way of thinking, and as a type of inquiry and which distinguish it from other types of inquiry such as science, theology, or art. I say "define" because we usually view these features *as essential* to the nature or identity of the philosophical discourse. What if I read a philosophical text, how do I know that the text I am reading is philosophical? Here I, first, assume that the essential features of the text are different from the essential features that define the nature of other *types of texts.* Second, the features that define the philosophical as such constitute the *essence* of the philosophical discourse as a type of thinking the way "tableness" defines or refers to the essence of the class of tables or to the essential features that distinguish them as a class. Thus, as a noun, "philosophicalness" refers to the features that define the essential nature of the philosophical as such and contradistinguishes it from the features that define the literary as such. Adding "ness" to "philosophical" or "literary" is consistent with a common practice in philosophy. This practice began with Plato and Aristotle some centuries ago. Moreover, using "philosophicalness" and "literariness" brings into relief the features that define the literary work and those that define the philosophical work. Awareness of this difference is urgently needed because much of the analysis I shall undertake revolves around the contrast and between these two types of work.

Third, significant form. Let me at once state that by "significant form" I mean "meaningful form," the kind of form that expresses or communicates human meaning. As I shall explain in detail in the first two chapters, the realm of human meaning is the realm of human values: as an ideal, value is a potential meaning, while meaning is realized value. The medium in and through which the literary work communicates values is the artistic dimension of the work, viz., its significant form, or the unity of the aesthetic qualities that inhere in the formal organization of the work. This dimension comes to life in the aesthetic experience as an aesthetic object, and this object unfolds in the experience as *a world of meaning*.

I am quitter aware that a large number of aestheticians shy away from the "significant form" which was coined by Clive Bel during the first decade of the past century. I do not subscribe to Bell's conception of art or to his interpretation of "significant form." I have borrowed the phrase "significant form" from him only because it communicates effectively my conception of the artistic and the aesthetic as basic categories in aesthetics, especially of explaining how values, or meaning, inhere in the artwork or how the artist imbues her work with meaning. Most, if not all, aestheticians would agree with me that the *meaning the artist creates inheres in the way she forms her medium*. But if an artist creates a form that express meaning, we should ask, *what* is this kind of form? How does it embody meaning? My answer to this question is that it is the kind of form that *signifies* meaning. But if it is the kind of form that *signifies* meaning, would it be odd, or unreasonable, to call it "significant form"? The question is not what we name this kind of form but what we mean, or understand, when we use it. I shall advance a detailed account of his concept.

STRUCTURE OF THE ARGUMENT

Is the philosophical novel as a genre possible? Yes. The thesis I advance and defend in this book is that the philosophical novel as a genre possible. The argument I advance in support of this thesis is composed of the following steps each one of which is a proposition. *First*, theme is the principle of genre distinction in literature; that is, the genre of a novel is determined by its dominant theme. For example, a novel is romantic if its dominant theme is romance, mystery if its dominant theme is mystery, or religious if its dominant theme is religion. I here assume that a literary novel may contain several themes but that its dominant theme is the basis of its genre identity. *Second*, possession of aesthetic qualities is the principle artistic distinction: an artifact is a work of art inasmuch as it possesses aesthetic qualities. It is a literary novel inasmuch as it possesses aesthetic qualities. Thus, the artistic dimension of the literary work is at the same time its artistic dimension: a novel is a literary work inasmuch it is an artwork. *Third,* unlike the story whose theme is directly given in the story we read, the theme of the literary novel is not directly given in the story we read but exists as potentiality in its formal organization; it comes to life as a literary work when we read it aesthetically. *Fourth,* and a corollary to the preceding proposition, the theme of a literacy novel inheres in the literary dimension of the novel, that is, in the unique form the artist creates in the artistic process. *Fifth,* a literary novel is philosophical if its theme centers on human value or on a slice of meaning. This proposition will be discussed in detail in the following two chapters. *Sixth,* since philosophical knowledge is conceptual, propositional, and since the knowledge communicated by a philosophical novel is neither conceptual nor propositional but depictive, the question arises: How does a literary novel communicates philosophical knowledge? Can philosophical knowledge be depicted? I argue that the vehicle of communicating philosophical knowledge in a literary work is metaphor. *Seventh,* what is metaphor? How does it communicate philosophical knowledge? I begin the discussion of this question with an analysis of a theory of metaphor and then illustrate by concrete example how a philosophical novel communicates knowledge.

Explanation of the Structure of the Argument

The purpose of the preceding outline of the propositions that make up the structure of the argument I shall advance in defending the thesis that philosophical novel is a literary genre is primarily to show as clearly as possible that the discussion of the various concepts and propositions which make the structure of this book is both *logically and conceptually* coherent, that is, the argument of the book stands on its own feet. It is extremely difficult to say that a literary novel can be philosophical if we cannot explain how its theme inheres in it and how it communicates philosophical knowledge.

I begin my discussion with the question of genre distinction in general for two reasons. First, a discussion of this question will constitute the conceptual framework within which I shall analyze the central concepts and propositions of the argument. Second, it is extremely difficult to argue that philosophical novel is a literary type or that it is a genre on a par with the recognized genres in the sphere of the literary novel if we do not know the principle of genre distinction and the way it functions in the evaluation of the genre-status of new or even existing literary genres. I tend to think that an explanation of this principle is a necessary condition for establishing the claim that philosophical novel is a literary genre.

The first essential concept in need of critical analysis is *literariness:* What makes a novel a literary work of art? I raise this question because, as I have just pointed out, the literary novel is a story, but not every story is a literary work of art. Thus, we should ask: What makes a novel a work of art? We can reasonably say, as I shall argue, that the presence of aesthetic qualities in a novel is what makes it a work of art. Put differently, possession of aesthetic qualities is the principle of literary distinction. But what are aesthetic qualities? What is their mode of existence? They do not exist in the plastic and temporal artworks, nor in the literary artworks, as ready-made realities but as potentialities inherent in the artwork as a significant form, as a form that embodies values, or meaning. This form constitutes the fabric of the aesthetic dimension, or stratum, of the work. This dimension emerges as an *aesthetic object* in the process of experiencing the work aesthetically. This object is, in turn, a world of meaning. I emphasize this point because the theme of the literary novel inheres as a potentiality in the novel *qua* significant form. I do not experience the theme when I read the novel as a story! The aesthetic dimension is the means by which the novel communicates its theme. Accordingly, if the philosophical novel is cognitive, the aesthetic object is the vehicle of communicating its philosophical knowledge. This is why I shall discuss in some detail literariness and the conditions under which it functions as a vehicle of knowledge.

But what is the identity of this vehicle in the philosophical novel? How can a philosophical concept or a process of reasoning inhere, or exist, as a unity of aesthetic qualities? If a literary novel communicates knowledge, if the aesthetic dimension, which comes to life as an aesthetic object, is the medium in which the knowledge is communicated, if this medium is not conceptual or propositional in character, how does the magical wand of the literary novelist transform the conceptual or propositional knowledge of the philosopher into an image, a scene, or an immediate presence, or, how does it exist in an aspectual or qualitative mode of being? My answer to this question is *metaphor.* This figure of speech is the medium in and through which the literary novel communicates philosophical knowledge.

Again we ask: What is metaphor? An analysis of this concept is crucially important for understanding the conditions under which a literary novel can be philosophical.

I conclude my discussion of the possibility of the philosophical novel as a genre with an analysis of Aristotle's theory of metaphor. I rely on his conception of metaphor only because it provides a clear account of the *ontic structure* of metaphor. According to this account, metaphor consists of ground, or subject, and carrier, or vehicle: "A is B." "A" is the ground and "B" is the carrier. The ground does not convey new ideas but the vehicle does. The ground points to the vehicle, which is the carrier of new ideas. I analyze two metaphors in two philosophical novels and one in a philosophical work, the Grand Inquisitor scene in Dostoevsky's *The Brothers Karamazov*, Plato's *Allegory of the Cave*, and Tolstoy's *The Death of Ivan Ilych*. The emphasis in this analysis is on how metaphor communicates philosophical knowledge.

But it is not enough to show that a literary novel can communicate philosophical knowledge; it is also necessary to ascertain that the knowledge communicated is true, certain, or sound. The means by which the philosopher establishes the truth and certainty of her knowledge is argument, demonstration, explanation, and critical analysis. But the philosophical novelist does not argue or analyze, nor does she try to establish the truth or certainty of the knowledge she communicates. She simply presents it. The book concludes with a detailed discussion of the concept of truth and certainty in philosophy and the philosophical novel.

Acknowledgments I would like to extend my gratitude to the editor of *Philosophy and Literature* for permitting me to include "Basis of Genre in the Philosophical Novel," Palgrave Macmillan, 2021 (forthcoming), as Chap. 2 and to the editor of *The Philosophy* Journal for using "The Basis Genre in Literature," vol. 13, number 1, as a part of Chap. 1.

REFERENCES AND SUGGESTED BIBLIOGRAPHY

Ingarden, Roman (1973). *The Literary Work of Art, Evanston*. Iniana: Northewestern University Press.

Kuczynska, Alicja (2018). *Art as a Philosophy*, in *Dialogue and Universalism*, issue 28; (1988); "Qualities of Things and Aesthetic qualities," in Mitias (1988), *Aesthetic Quality and Aesthetic Experience*.

CHAPTER 2

Basis of Genre in the Literary Novel

INTRODUCTION

Most aestheticians and literary critics agree that the domain of a literary novel is composed of different genres, such as mystery, horror, romance, or fantasy, and that this domain is open-ended, in the sense that it is possible for new genres and sub-genres to emerge in the near or distant future. Indeed, it is difficult for a person to buy or read a literary novel that cannot be included in one of the generally recognized genres. Moreover, it is agreed that *theme* forms the basis of distinguishing one type of literary genre from another. For example, a novel is classified as a "romantic novel" if its theme is romance. However, what is the *ontological status* of theme in a literary novel? How does it make its appearance in the aesthetic experience? Under what conditions can one identify the genre identity of a novel? To what extent is theme an "objectively" given reality?

My aim in raising these questions is not to query or dispute the existing classification of literary novels into genres, but to provide an epistemological and ontological explanation regarding the basis of genre distinction in literary novels. It is one thing to say that *Wuthering Heights* is a romantic novel, while it is something entirely different to examine the *rationale* behind this assertion, that is, to understand the principle by which it is categorized as romantic. Is it romantic because the plot revolves around a passionate love affair between a man and a woman? A romantic novel is a love story, but not every love story is necessarily a romantic novel. Many

© The Author(s), under exclusive license to Springer Nature Switzerland AG 2022
M. H. Mitias, *The Philosophical Novel as a Literary Genre*, https://doi.org/10.1007/978-3-030-97385-8_2

novels contain meaningful, enlightening, and dramatic love affairs, and some contain meaningful discourses on the nature of love, without necessarily being romantic.

We may, broadly speaking, say that theme provides the basis of genre distinction in the literary novel. This is a reasonable proposal, and I shall discuss it in some detail in the following pages, but it is not as clear as it seems. Although a plot may revolve around a love affair, a religious experience, or an exotic adventure and may give the impression that it is a romantic, religious, or adventure novel, it may not necessarily qualify for inclusion in the romantic, religious, or adventure genre since it may *veil a deeper, more central theme*. For example, the plot in Tolstoy's *The Death of Ivan Ilych* revolves around the rise and death of a successful and respected magistrate, but in fact, the theme of the novel deals with the meaning of human life (Porter 2004). Again, although the plot constitutes the structure of the literary novel and frequently functions as the ontological *locus* of its theme, it cannot be the basis of genre distinction. This is based on the fundamental assumption that a literary novel is not merely a story. A story can be emotionally attractive, thrilling, or juicy without being a literary novel. The structure, purpose, and mode of existence of the story are different from the structure, purpose, and mode of existence of the literary novel. Albeit a narrative, the story is given as a ready-made object. It is the narrative we read; put differently, it is identical to the narrative we read. Even the psychological revelations made by the characters, the events, or the narrator are descriptive in nature. Indeed, what we imagine or conceive when we read the story are to a large extent based on what we read in the text. This is one of the reasons why it would be reasonable to say that the plot of the story forms the basis of its genre identity. Therefore, it would be a romantic or horror story if the theme of its plot consists of predominantly romantic or horror elements.

In spotlighting the difference between a story and a literary novel, I do not in any way underrate the value of the story or the role it plays in culture, imagination, or human life. My comparison is purely descriptive, not evaluative. Like the novel, the story presents a distinctive nature and purpose while meeting a particular aesthetic need. I would venture to say that, overall, stories are more in demand than literary novels. Can we underestimate the role stories play in cultivating the minds of children, as well as adults? Can we easily forget the stories our parents read to us when we are young? Can we ignore the essential function stories perform in the world of entertainment and information? Do teachers, religious leaders, and parents not use stories as a medium of explanation and raising questions?

However, unlike the story, the literary novel is not, *as a literary work*, identical to its plot, although the plot may play a decisive role in the development of its theme, but *a potentiality inherent in it*. Moreover, any evaluative statement we make about the story can be corroborated by direct reference to the narrative. There is no need to venture beyond the text to ascertain that it is beautiful, interesting, or good. Is this why many people read stories in a short time, why most stories do not leave a deep impression or impact upon the way we think, feel, or act, or why a large number of people read stories mainly to kill time or simply to have a pleasant experience? But the plot is not identical to the novel as a literary work of art and is not, in itself, the basis or the direct bearer of its aesthetic value. Do we appreciate the *Mona Lisa* simply because it is the representation of a woman we happen to like or because we are interested in its features on a historical or technical level? Do we read Dostoevsky's *The Idiot* simply because it is the story of a bungler or because it signifies a sick man who cannot see his way through the maze of nineteenth-century Russian society? Do we appreciate Brancusi's *Bird in Flight* simply because it is a figurine that fits in a specific place on the mantelpiece? Do we attend a performance of *Oedipus the King* simply to watch a king who foolishly ignores the advice of a blind wise man, plucks his eyes out of their sockets, ruins his family, and abandons his throne? Of course not, primarily because these are works of art.

As I have just pointed out, a literary novel is not only a story; more importantly, it is a work of art. But, what makes it art? I raise this question because its artistic dimension is the ontological locus of its theme. However, this dimension is not given as a ready-made reality the way its scenes, characters, or events are given but as a potentiality inherent in the novel as a *significant form*, that is, in the *way* the plot is arranged as a story (see Bell 1958; Mitias 1987). In this context, we can say that the significant form of the novel is tethered to, or embedded in, the story. The significant form provides the foundation of the novel as a literary work of art. It is what the artist aims at during the creative process and what the reader aims at during the process of reading the novel aesthetically. It is significant because it signifies meaning. *The literary novel is a world of meaning* (see Dufrenne 1973). This world is and should be the object of literary appreciation and criticism. Tolstoy did not write *The Death of Ivan Ilych* to describe the death of an important government functionary, a man we frequently see walking in the streets of social life, but rather to disclose an essential dimension regarding the meaning of human life. The vehicle of this disclosure is the theme the form embodies or communicates. This theme emerges as a world distinct, but not separable, from the story as a significant form primarily because it inheres in it, in the sense that it exists in, or permeates, its very structure.

Now, if theme forms the basis of genre distinction in a literary novel, if the ontological locus of this theme is the literary dimension of the literary novel, if this dimension is not given as a ready-made reality but comes into being during the process of reading it aesthetically, and finally, if the differentiae which define the thematic identity emerges from the womb of the *literary dimension* of the novel, it would necessarily follow that an understanding of the basis of genre distinction in a literary novel should proceed from a reasonable analysis of (a) the literary dimension of the novel and (b) the conditions under which types of theme are embodied in the novel and realized in the aesthetic experience of the reader. This proposal is based on the assumption that the theme is often not provided directly in the structure of the novel as a story but as a work of art. Accordingly, an examination of how a story communicates the theme inherent in it as a significant form presupposes an inquiry into the sense in which a novel is a literary work of art. But fulfilling this condition is not enough; we should also explore the nature of the particular theme whose presence in a group of novels distinguishes that group as a genre. Here we can ask: What determines whether a group of novels belongs to the romance, horror, or fantasy genre? Finding an answer to this question is urgent primarily because the differentiae that distinguish the group as a genre reside in the artistic dimension of the novel: Under what conditions can this be realized in the aesthetic experience? The point, which calls for special attention here, is that neither the theme nor the differentiae can be fully understood without an adequate account of the artistic structure of the literary novel and how it emerges during the aesthetic experience.

In this chapter, I shall, first, discuss the literary dimension of the literary novel: What makes a novel a literary work of art? Here, I shall argue that the literary novel is a world of meaning and that the main characters, actions, scenes, and events are essentially aesthetic qualities that can be expressed in different figures of speech such as metaphors, similes, or symbolic images. Second, I shall discuss the possibility of articulating the basic features of a theme into *differentiae* that can act as the basis of genre distinction in a literary novel. Finally, I shall illustrate this possibility by an examination of a philosophical novel.

Literariness

What makes a novel a *literary* work? This question asks for the feature or aspect whose presence in the novel makes it a literary work. What is the mode of existence of this feature or aspect? How does it belong to the novel? If the literary novel is more than a story, it must be more than a descriptive narrative—what is this "more"? It cannot be supervenient to the structure of the given text, but an integral part of it; otherwise, we would not be able to experience the literary novel, *qua* integrity, as a literary work, and we would not be able to justify its inclusion in the genre of a literary novel. The identity of an object, regardless of whether it is physical, biological, or human, is determined by reference to its essential structure, or features, not by something external or superadded to it.

Art, I submit, is the principle of literary distinction. Accordingly, a novel is a literary work inasmuch as it is art. I say "inasmuch as" because (a) the art-making element is not given as a ready-made reality but as a possibility for infinite realization in the aesthetic experience, and (b) if this element is a ready-made reality, we would undercut the possibility of aesthetic evaluation; that is, we would not be able to judge works as good or better, more or less beautiful, excellent or mediocre. The aesthetic value of an artwork depends on the extent to which its artistic dimension is rich, profound, or spiritually uplifting. Art is also what distinguishes a literary novel from a story. Only when the novel acquires an artistic being, does it become a literary work (see Dufrenne 1973; Ingarden 1973; Mitias 1987).

We can now ask: What makes an artifact, such as a painting or a symphony, art? *Possession of aesthetic qualities*; the unity of these qualities is what I call in this paper "significant form." This kind of form is symbolic in nature and, like all symbols, embodies or signifies a content of meaning that transcends its given parameters. We do not imagine, conceive, or see this content in the symbol but based on certain rules and conventions, we can make a transition to the content of meaning signified by it. However, although this content is not identical to the symbol, it cannot exist apart from it separately, nor can it be superadded to it, mainly due to the signification being embedded in the symbol. This is why, during the process of transitioning from the symbol to its signification, the symbol becomes an ingredient of the signification (see Langer 1951; Cassirer 1962).

It is a generally recognized fact by philosophers and scientists that the aim of the scientist is to know *the facts* constituting the scheme of nature and, if possible, nature as a whole while the aim of the philosopher and the artist is to know the *meaning of these facts*. While the facts of nature are given as objects of empirical observation, the meaning is articulated based on the knowledge disclosed by the scientist. The scientist's knowledge of matter, life, and consciousness plays a decisive role in how we understand ourselves as human beings, how we design our life-projects, how we treat other human beings, how we understand the nature and purpose of the cosmic process, or how we interpret the meaning of justice, freedom, love, and happiness. In contrast to the realm of facts, the realm of meaning is the realm of human values—truth, beauty, and goodness. The first embraces values such as wisdom, erudition, and good sense; the second embraces values such as justice, love, and honesty; and the third embraces values such as elegance, grandeur, and gracefulness. To this list, we may add metaphysical and religious values. The first embraces values such as freedom, the purpose, and meaning of existence in general, and human life in particular, while the second embraces values such as grace, faith, and piety. A quick, yet investigative, look at the domain of a literary novel will readily show that human values—their source, nature, and application—is the central theme of the novel.

Values are not natural facts; they are human constructs. They are ideals, and as ideals, they are schemas, plans for action at the individual and social levels in the cultural, social, economic, political, and technological spheres of human life. An ideal defines the essential nature of *a type* of action without either implying or referring to concrete, particular actions. For example, equality, fairness, or rightness defines the essential nature of the ideal of justice, but this definition is general and as such ideal; it states that every just action should exhibit equality, fairness, or rightness as its essential nature. The activity of translating the general into a particular action or type of action is the task of the individual, the jury, the judge, or the legislator. This is based on the assumption that no two situations in any area of human life—practical, theoretical, scientific, moral, artistic, or religious—are identical. What may be just, generous, wise, elegant, or appropriate in a particular situation may not be so in a different situation, culture, or historical period. Consider the value, or ideal, of divine love. Is there one specific way of loving God? Again, is there one way of loving human beings, creating beautiful objects, seeking freedom, discovering the truth, or pursuing happiness? Again, do we not discover new, deeper, or richer meaning in a novel when we read it repeatedly or as we grow older and hopefully wiser? Do teachers not frequently ask students to re-read a novel or a poem in the hope of penetrating their deeper meaning?

This point merits particular emphasis, not only because the type of values, which permeate the artistic dimension of the literary novel and make it literature, *is a wealth of potentiality* awaiting realization in the aesthetic experience, but also because it can be realized in different ways and degrees. How can we discover new meanings or even delve deeper into the depth of the literary novel if these meanings do not exist in the novel or if we do not believe that the novel is an inexhaustible source of meaning?

But how does value exist in the literary novel? This question aims at the sense in which a literary novel is a significant form, for, as stated earlier, possession of this kind of form is what makes it art and consequently a literary work of art. As a story I buy from the bookstore, the literary novel is a structure or a kind of formation; as such, it is a form. This form constitutes its foundation as a novel. If in some way it changes, the story changes, and if it collapses, the novel collapses. However, the novel is not merely a form; it is a significant form. It is not merely a story, but the kind of story that "hides" something, viz., meaning within its folds. I say "hide" because it is not given directly to our imagination, and yet it can be lured from its hiding place by the seductive power of its significant form in the event of assuming an aesthetic attitude and making a serious effort to read the novel aesthetically. This power resides in what aestheticians call "aesthetic qualities."

As I shall shortly discuss in some detail, their presence in an artifact is what makes it art, and their presence in the novel is what makes it a literary work of art! The birthplace of this form is the creative vision of the artist. The novelist does not create the words she uses in composing the novel; she creates a form, that is, a plot that embodies meaning. How can this kind of form embody meaning? The type of meaning intended in this context is not lexical or conceptual, nor the meaning of the novel as a narrative, but the type of meaning that inheres in the form as an organic unity and emerges in the aesthetic experience as an aesthetic object. The novel as an artwork undergoes a transformation of identity during the aesthetic experience; it becomes an *aesthetic object*. What is the ontological status of this object? Let me at once state that the meaning signified by the significant form inheres in the literary novel as a potentiality that can be actualized during the process of reading it aesthetically. This assertion calls for an explanation (see Mitias 1987).

The meaning communicated by the novel exists within the web of the aesthetic qualities that inhere as a potentiality in its significant form. The capacity of this kind of form to embody meaning, and to disclose it in the aesthetic experience, is magically transferred by the novelist's creative vision to the form she is trying to create. *This magic infuses and steers the way in which the form is created.* The uniqueness of this *way* and the magic of the hand that fashions it is what distinguish the novel from the story. It is what incites and gradually directs the imagination of the reader to the meaning implicit in the form. A novel that cannot perform this twofold function remains a story. Accordingly, when we say that meaning inheres as a potentiality in the literary novel, we should mean that its form has the capacity, *potential*, to communicate this meaning by virtue of its form. This meaning comes to life on the wings of the aesthetic qualities whose presence in the novel is what makes it art and, consequently, a literary work of art: a novel is a literary work inasmuch as it is art. Thus, any discourse about literariness is in effect a discourse about the artistic dimension of the novel, and any discourse about this dimension is, in turn, a discourse about the aesthetic qualities, which inheres in its significant form. The unity of these qualities, which appear in the aesthetic experience as an aesthetic object, constitute the structure of the novel as a literary work.

Generally, form is a whole composed of parts; it is a specific arrangement of individual elements—things, colors, lines, motions, shapes, words, and images—into a basic structure. Possession of form is a necessary condition for the existence and knowledge of an object, regardless of whether it is physical or mental. A formless object does not, and cannot, exist. We know it by means of its form, that is, by the way its elements are grouped into a structure. For example, Aristotle defined man (human being) as a rational animal. This means that the elements that make up the structure of the concept of man are animality and rationality. Knowledge of a human being would be the outcome of our knowledge of these two elements—their constituents and the way they are united into a whole. We can certainly inquire about the nature of animality and rationality. Like the concept of man, these two constituents are types of form; we know what they are by examining the elements that constitute their essential structure. The web of our knowledge of the objects, which comprise the physical and zoological worlds, is weaved from our knowledge of the structural forms that make up the design of these worlds. These objects are given to the scientist and the philosopher as ready-made objects. For example, we discover the formal structure of a rock, a tree, or a cat by analyzing it into its simpler parts; we accomplish this by sensuous observation, tools, experiments, and mathematical computation. However, human nature is not directly given to us, and it is not given as a ready-made object. But, although it is not given directly, we can construct a theory or a concept of its essential structure. This notion is based on the (a) direct observation of how we think, desire, make decisions, act, and exercise the activities of consciousness and self-consciousness, (b) the extent to which the values we seek as human beings foster human progress at the individual and social levels, (c) and the achievements of humanity during the past five millennia.

But unlike natural objects and even objects in the visual and auditory fine arts, the literary novel exists in a non-sensuous medium, namely, written and sometimes oral language. However, like the painter, the sculptor, or the musician, who does not create her medium, but forms it in a certain way, the novelist does not create the words she uses; she forms them in a certain way. As a symbolic medium, ordinary language communicates meaning conceptually. This type of language prevails in science and philosophy. However, the literary novelist uses this medium to create and communicate different, and sometimes higher, levels of meaning. She does not only create figures of speech such as allegory, simile, satire, irony, metaphor, and images, which express different types or dimensions of meaning, she also creates stories that embody *worlds of meaning*; these worlds defy philosophical or scientific conceptualization. How does the literary novel embody meaning?

I tend to think that the logic governing the creative process in the different art forms is one and the same. Ordinary language, which consists of words that are formed phonically and as written marks on paper, can be a medium of artistic expression. Let me elaborate this statement by two examples, the first is from the visual arts and the second is from the domain of the literary novel (Ingarden 1973). First, a preliminary remark is in order. As a means of expression, significant form is a kind of language mainly because, like ordinary language, it is *symbolic* in nature. But, unlike ordinary language, which communicates conceptual meaning in most of its uses, significant form communicates *human meaning*, the kind that instantiates *values* in the multitude of moral, religious, political, metaphysical, and cultural spheres of human experience. It is also important to point out that, unlike ordinary language, which is constructed according to certain rules and conventions, significant form is created according to the logic of the creative vision that illuminates the process of artistic creation. This is why it is possible to say that the artist creates rather than follows specific rules in this kind of activity. But, although the artwork is the outcome of a creative vision, one that comes into being *sui generis*, the intuition and articulation of the meaning inherent in it is neither arbitrary nor idiosyncratic. This is primarily due to its creation being governed by the logic that steers the creative process, on the one hand, and the logic of the kind of meaning the artist seeks to communicate, on the other. This twofold logic forms the basis of learning how to penetrate the meaning implicit in the different art forms and works. Is this not the kind of logic relied upon by art teachers in teaching students how to appreciate works of music, painting, literature, dance, or sculpture? Do we not gradually master the dynamics of this logic in the activity of experiencing artworks as we grow intellectually, socially, culturally, and emotionally? This is based on the assumption that art teachers, critics, art historians, and lovers of art are, to a reasonable extent, conversant in the logic that underlies aesthetic appreciation and evaluation in the different art forms.

Now, just as the formal structure of a painting, for example, DaVinci's *Mona Lisa*, can be a symbolic form that communicates a world of meaning, a literary novel, which is presented to us as a linguistic structure, can also be a symbolic form that communicates a world of meaning. The object that welcomes my eyes when I approach this painting with the intention of perceiving it aesthetically is the representation of a woman looking abstractly into infinite space. I may like or dislike the representation. In this case, my reaction is based on how it affects my ordinary sensibility: what I see is what I like or dislike. This is what DaVinci painted on the canvas, after all! My ordinary eyes do not interpret or judge what I see *aesthetically*.

However, my imagination is the seat of aesthetic appreciation, evaluation, and judgment. If I linger before the painting and contemplate the representation critically, reflecting on the relations between the different lines, colors, and the representation as a whole, and suddenly find myself attracted to the eyes—to their look, to their meditativeness, to their focus on an indefinable space, indeed, to an infinite space, a space that seems to confront her eyes as a challenge—yes, if I undergo this type of reflective contemplation, I suddenly discover that I am abandoning my ordinary mode of perception, and assuming what aestheticians and art critics call "aesthetic attitude," in which my vision moves from the representation as a given form to what it signifies, that is, it moves from seeing the representation as a given form to seeing it as a significant form. This change in attitude marks the transition from the ordinary to the aesthetic mode of perception, from perceiving the painting as a *picture* of a woman to perceiving it as a *work of art* (see Mitias 1987). In this mode of perception, my vision moves dialectically between the source of the look and its object. Its source is the eyes of the woman, indeed her soul, and its object is the infinite space. The eyes are absorbed, perhaps lost, in this space, and we can conjecture that they are trying to discover some secret in it—perhaps its origin. Indirectly, the interest of the woman in that space becomes my interest; her meditative look becomes my meditative look. But, then, can her look, mine, or the look of any other human being fathom that infinity? Can it comprehend it? Is losing oneself in this kind of space wise? But my eyes do not stop there; they move to the face of the woman. My vision dances on the rope that connects the finite with the infinite, the finite human being and the infinite space, only to be thrust dialectically from one pole of being (the finite) to the other pole (the infinite). The finite pole desires to know the secret of its existence, which is a marvel, but a confounding marvel. However, the infinite pole cannot fulfill this desire, which is reasonable, painfully reasonable. How can the *mind* of the finite comprehend the *being* of the infinite? But, if it cannot comprehend it, how can it make sense of its existence: Why do I exist? Why should my existence be a ripple in the cosmic process? How should I live in this transient life? I do not raise these and similar questions when I am performing my dance on that rope; on the contrary, the dance drags them from the recesses of my subconscious mind to the active domain of my conscious mind. Here I understand their meaning clearly. In this dance, I am not merely a viewer but also a participant, because the meditative eyes that gape into the infinite space and the dance they perform on the rope that connects the two modes of being are my eyes and my dance, and the questions they raise are my questions. I do not merely think them; I *see* them, and I intuit them, in those eyes!

But this disturbing realization, which expands the field of my aesthetic perception, only because the representation as a whole is an organic unity, gently directs my attention to the lips of the woman—to those magically formed lips! It is impossible to observe them as lips without perceiving the baffling, hypnotizing, and disturbing smile. The smile oozes with *enigma*! How can I, or anyone else, stand still or remain silent before an enigma that rises from the depth of the human soul? Moreover, why does it rise from Mona Lisa's soul? I am inclined to think that it rises from her soul because her lips are having a dialogue with her eyes. The enigma I see, and read, in the smile must be the same enigma Mona Lisa feels when she discovers that the secret she is seeking in the depth of that infinity will forever remain hidden in that depth. How would you feel if the most urgent and most perplexing questions, relating to the source and purpose of your life, cannot be answered? Confused? Forlorn? Gasping for a breath of life, of light? There is no need for me to continue my aesthetic visit to this painting. I hope that what I said has shed some light of understanding on how a world of meaning that inheres as a potentiality in the significant form of a visual work of art can emerge in the aesthetic experience as a world of meaning.

I can now proceed to a discussion of how a literary novel embodies a world of meaning and how this world unfolds in the aesthetic experience. But it is important to indicate at the outset that, unlike the visual or auditory work of art whose significant form inheres in a physical medium, the significant form of the literary novel inheres in a linguistic, conceptual medium (Ingarden 1973). This medium exists in the subjective experience of the reader. This difference separating the literary works of art from the visual and auditory works of art is, in principle, negligible mainly because the story in which the literary dimension inheres as a potentiality for realization is an objectively given structure. It is founded in the plot of the story. The objectivity of the plot is not given in any greater or lesser degree than the objectivity of the representation of a painting or the sculpture I see with my eyes in a museum. I shall now illustrate this point by a brief analysis of Tolstoy's *The Death of Ivan Ilych*, and I shall discuss I in greater detail in Chap. 4.

The physical book titled *The death of Ivan Ilych*, which sits on the top shelf of my bookcase, is not, strictly speaking, the novel Tolstoy wrote. We can tear it to shreds, and we can burn it. Destroying this book does not amount to a destruction of the novel because there are other copies of it and because the meaning of the words, which make up the text, does not ontologically exist on the pages of the book, but come into existence in the mind of the reader during the process of reading the novel. The marks I see on those pages are no more than signifiers that point to some content—ideas, images, figures of speech, anecdotes, or relations—formed in a certain way. We have to be familiar with the rules that govern the use of such signifiers, which we begin to learn in elementary school, and then move to what they signify or refer to. We may metaphorically view these marks as "shells" or vehicles that contain or convey content of meaning. We can move to the level of meaning and comprehend it only if we master the rules and conventions according to which they are arranged. They are usually subsumed under the categories of grammar and syntax (see Bailey 1975).

As a story, the literary novel is an objectively given structure inasmuch as it is constructed according to recognized literary and grammatical syntactical rules and practices. How does such a structure embody a world of meaning? I think that it embodies such a world when the story in which it is founded is, as I argued earlier, a significant form. It is vital to point out here that just as the representation in *Mona Lisa* embodies a significant form, and just as the representation as a work of art exists for the sake of the world of meaning potentially contained within it as a significant form, the story we read in *The Death of Ivan Ilych* is a significant form and exists for the sake of the world of meaning inherent in it. This work is a story about an important government official, Ivan Ilych, who is married to a socially respected and well to do woman, esteemed by his colleagues and social class, and is in possession of the conditions of happiness. At the peak of his success as a magistrate and as a socialite, he gets sick. At first, he ignores his sickness, considering it a minor ailment that will soon pass. But it does not; on the contrary, it festers and gradually develops into a fatally threatening malady. He seeks medical help, but neither the doctor who attends to him nor anyone else can stop the development of his illness. At first, he smells the scent of Death and then begins to imagine him lying in wait around the corner of his house. He struggles agonizingly with Death's impending arrival: How can he face him, much less surrender his soul to him? How can he leave the life he loves so much? During the last three weeks of his life, especially in the last three days, Ivan experiences the most excruciating pain a human being can bear. During this period, he discovers that the life he lived was a sham and that all the people around him, except the peasant Gerasim, who nurses him silently and quietly, and his son, who is still a flare of innocent youth, are selfish, mean, and drowning in a sea of lies and social hypocrisy. Tolstoy tells us at the beginning of the novel that "The past history of Ivan Ilych's life was the most simple and eventful, and yet most terrible" (in Porter 2004, p. 261). But underlying, and indeed permeating, the story is a profound theme: *the meaning of human life*. How should I live my life in this world? Under what existential conditions can my life be worth living? Can I justify the life I have lived when I reach the end, the very end? These questions are only the headlines of the theme. The question that merits special attention here is what makes the story Tolstoy wrote a significant form, one that signifies this theme? What enables me as a reader to make a transition from the novel as a story to it as *a literary work, that is,* how can I make a transition to the world of meaning inherent in it? Tolstoy did not raise these questions, nor did he suggest a way for making this transition. The key to this transition lies in its significant form, in the way he weaved the story.

The novel does not begin with a narration of the history of Ivan's life, marriage, professional and social success, sickness, agony unto death, and then his actual death. It begins with his funeral. A funeral home is a place where a person—a dead one—spends the last few hours of his or her sojourn on this earth. The smell of death flows from the face of the dead man with the nastiest scent you can imagine! Who can avoid inhaling it then and hear his stomach cry with disgust against it? Yet, everyone in that room is pretending they smell the scent of the beautiful flowers that cover the coffin and other parts of the room and showing their love to the man they have loved and admired. They are in denial about the reality of death and the imminent prospect of their own death. In adopting this attitude, they assume that this monster will devour the other—the enemy, the friend, the neighbor, the coworker, everyone else—but not "me." Is this why they are discussing everything else—money, social gossip, the latest news—but not their mortality and certainly not death. In short, the funeral ceremony is reduced to a social event! However, the novel concludes with a profound psychoanalytical account of the actual scene of Ivan's death. This scene vividly discloses but does not discursively recount the horrible, trenchant, and debilitating encounter with death. Implied in this focus on the annihilation of one's life is the intimate relation between the question of death and the question of the meaning of human life: if life is short, if our destiny consists of a continual process of human growth and development, which is a most daunting challenge, if this short life is all we have, how should we live it? How can we face the moment of death courageously, peacefully, and with a clear conscience?

Tolstoy did not write this story simply to describe how a man dies a pathetic death, because we encounter more pathetic, more confounding, more disturbing scenes of death during the course of ordinary life than the scene of Ivan's death. He wrote this novel to disclose the significance of death in our lives. Moreover, he spotlighted the scene of death in this novel primarily to direct our attention to the importance of the question of the meaning of human life: How can a genuine human being, one who is cultivated morally, intellectually, aesthetically, and socially lead a fake life, a life of deception the way Ivan did? How can she neglect to meet her needs as a human individual? Is there a question more important than the question of the meaning of human life?

The death scene brings into vivid relief a contrast striking between two facts: the fact of human mortality and the general tendency of people to ignore it, on the one hand, and the fact that they live their lives superficially, hypercritical, and foolishly, on the other. This contrast is not communicated to the reader discursively but presented to her as a depiction, as a luminous presence. Once she contemplates this presence and continues to read the novel, can she anymore read the novel as a story? The mere vision of this contrast triggers a change of attitude, from reading the novel as a story to reading it as a literary work. The literary dimension, and along with the real theme, gradually unfolds and reaches a dramatic point in the last three chapters when Ivan stands on the edge of being and sees the depth of his own non-being.

My critic would now interject: your analysis of *The Death of Ivan Ilych* has illuminated the conditions under which the theme of the literary novel, which exists as a potentiality in its significant form, becomes a living dimension of meaning in the aesthetic experience. You have also referred to this dimension as a world *and* as "world of meaning." How do we experience this dimension as a world? What makes it a world? This is a fair question.

First, the characters, events, and scenes within which the action of the novel takes place are not shadowy but substantial objects. Although Ivan does not exist in the real world, and although he exists as a potentiality in the novel, which is an abstract type of existence, he comes to life as a real human being during the reading process, and this reality is sometimes more substantial than the reality of the objects that fill our social and natural environment—at home, in the workplace, or in the streets of the social life. His pain, anxiety, agony, questions, guilt, screams, and passion for life are not simply abstract mental states; they are living objects and events in my mind, heart, and will. I do not experience Ivan as a shadowy object out there in a vista of my imagination, but as a real human being with whom ordinary people can interact and understand. When I am reading the novel aesthetically, I *empathize* with him; I become a possible Ivan. He forces me to look at myself in the mirror of truth. I cannot ignore the questions his predicament provokes in my mind, even though I may refuse to feel that I am another Ivan. Do we not sometimes suddenly notice that we are shaking our heads, pursing our lips, blushing, laughing, frowning, or feeling sad, joyful, or confused in the process of reading a literary novel?

Similarly, the scenes and events that make up the tapestry of the novel come to life in the activity of reading it aesthetically. For example, the funeral scene with which the novel begins is as real as the myriad scenes we encounter in real funeral homes. The corpse, friends, family members, flowers, and music are instantiations of real corpses, friends, family members, flowers, and music we encounter in real funeral homes. Although we do not encounter a scene identical to this one in real life, it is *true to real life*—to how people say farewell to a dead man, how they view death, how they gossip at funeral homes, how funerals are more about the living than the dead. Additionally, they are true to life, not only because Tolstoy discloses the essence of such a scene, which the philosopher can do conceptually, but primarily because the *way* he disclosed it endowed the novel with the capacity to become a luminous presence in the experience of the reader. The ability to endow images, scenes, or descriptions with this kind of capacity is the secret of the creative imagination. This secret lies in the capacity to infuse these images, scenes, or descriptions with life.

Second, as a significant form, the literary novel is an indeterminate reality. It is not merely the story the novelist writes; it is the significant form that inheres in it. As a literary work, the novel can be read differently at different times, by different readers, and from different perspectives. No two identical readings of the novel are possible, not only because the psychological, intellectual, and cultural knowledge and skills of the reader are always changing, not only because the significant form is weaved out of a multiplicity of meanings, but also because the novel is an inexhaustible source of meaning. This is one main reason why we can characterize the literary novel *as a world of meaning*. As I emphasized earlier, value is a schema, a plan for action; as such, it is a fountain of possible realizations.

We enjoy reading the literary novel because it is written beautifully or aesthetically. Beauty is an intrinsic value. We seek it as an end in itself, not as a means to an end. This value manifests itself in the way the novelist chooses the plot, the language she uses, the images she creates, the figures of speech she employs to express the elusive feelings, emotions, and meanings, the way she depicts the scenes, and the way she presents the theme of the novel. These parts do not exist in it discretely but as an organic unity, so do their beauty and the beauty of the work as a whole. However, as realized meaning, beauty is not a particular object of any kind; accordingly, it is indefinable. Can we describe the beauty we feel when we listen to a beautiful piece of music or contemplate a magnificent sunset? Can we describe the love we feel when we are in the heat of union with the beloved? The beauty of a work of art is the spiritual air that radiates from the form of the work as an organic unity; we breathe it the way we breathe

the air of spiritual life. It flows from this form the way light flows from the sun as an inexhaustible abundance. Do we not delve deeper into the beauty of a sunset the more we contemplate the physical and cosmic dynamics that underlie it? Do we not discover newer and more profound meaning when we read *Moby Dick, Middle March,* or *Of Human Bondage,* as we grow older? Do we not enjoy the beauty of a man or a woman when we know that the beauty we perceive with our eyes reflects inner intellectual and moral beauty? Can we define this kind of beauty—its charm, profundity, warmth? Even these three epithets are a metaphorical way of referring to it! Beauty is seductive! It lures the reader into the heart of the novel the way the beauty of a woman lures the heart of a man into her heart or the way the beauty of a man lures a woman into his heart. It plays an active role in changing the reader's attitude from the mode of ordinary perception to the mode of aesthetic appreciation.

But we do not usually read novels simply because they are beautiful but mainly because they are morally, intellectually, and spiritually meaningful. I do not exaggerate if I say that the meaning we experience in them is a concretization of a rich mosaic of human values: religious, moral, metaphysical, cultural, and aesthetic. Let us venture another look at *The Death of Ivan Ilych.* As a value, human life is the dominant theme of the novel. This value is unusually complex because it is composed of a cluster of social, political, aesthetic, moral, and intellectual values. We encounter these values in the major scenes of this novel: in the workplace, home, social life, Ivan's relationships with his colleagues, his wife, his doctor, his children, and his peasant. Every value that underlies these scenes is, as I argued earlier, a potentiality for a multitude of realizations in different ways and degrees. The more we read this novel aesthetically and reflectively, the deeper we glide into the womb of this potentiality. I tend to think that the desire to enjoy meaning is a fundamental urge in human nature.

Third, the theme of the literary novel comes to life in the aesthetic experience as an aesthetic object (Ingarden 1973). As I indicated earlier, the aesthetic object is the aim of the novelist during the process of artistic creation and the aim of the reader during the process of reading it. The aesthetic object is a world of meaning. It does not derive its being and identity from an external source; it is an independent and individual sphere of meaning. This is another reason why we can refer to it as "world." The meaning we experience in it originates from the values that dominate the theme of the novel. When I read *The Death of Ivan Ilych,* I discover what it means to face death and how this phenomenon provokes the question of the meaning of human life; I also see the urgent need to come to grips with this question. In this discovery, I do not avail myself of any external source but rely exclusively on the life that unfolds before my mind as I read the novel. It seems that Tolstoy planted the seeds of the theme of the novel in the first chapter. These seeds grow and become a tree in the course of reading it. In fact, the story that unfolds in my experience becomes my story because, in the act of reading it, I am its author. I am the agent that brings it to life. Paradoxically, I become captive to its world. Can it be otherwise if I am one with it while I am reading it?

We make a grave mistake if we view the aesthetic object as a reality independent of the medium the artist used in the process of creating her work, namely, the novel that sits on the shelf of my bookcase for two reasons. First, as a text, the book embodies the aesthetic object as a significant form: the aesthetic object exists in the significant form as a potentiality. Expressed metaphorically, this form inhabits the medium in which it inheres. It cannot be experienced or conceived separate from it. It is, after all, the way this medium is formed! Accordingly, if the significant form is the unity of the aesthetic qualities which make up the structure of the significant form, these qualities can be realized only in their medium *qua* significant form. Second, regardless of whether it is physical or conceptual, this medium is spiritualized in the aesthetic experience, because in reading the novel aesthetically we do not experience it merely as a story but also as a meaningful story, a story imbued with realized aesthetic qualities: elegance, love, joy, justice, freedom, or tragedy. This is based on the assumption that the phenomenon of experience cannot be reduced to a physiological, conceptual, or psychological event. Am I aware of the physical painting when I am experiencing *Mona Lisa* aesthetically? Am I aware of any concepts or images when I am reading *The Death of Ivan Ilych* aesthetically? In this sort of experience, the human self rises to its highest level of spiritual realization. It is, I think, appropriate to say that during this event I am a drop of experience, as Whitehead would say, and that this event is spiritual in nature. I say "spiritual" because it includes the physical, psychological, and conceptual elements that form the substance of the experience, but as an organic unity. The experience of the whole is always more than the mathematical sum of its parts.

It should be clear from the preceding discussion in its entirety that if the basis of *literary distinction is art,* if the basis of artistic distinction is possession of aesthetic qualities, if significant form is the unity of these qualities, if their unity constitutes the structure of the aesthetic object, if this object is a world of meaning, then it should follow that a novel that is a literary work embodies such an object. I have discussed the constituents of this line of reasoning mainly to show that the literary dimension of the novel exists in it. If a novel is a literary work of art, it should declare its literariness from within, from the depth of its artistic structure, not by the judgment of an external authority, and if an authority makes such a judgment, it should be based on this kind of declaration.

Theme as the Basis of Genre in the Literary Novel

I think the time is ripe to ask: What is the basis of genre in the literary novel, for example, is it a romance, horror, or fantasy novel? In answering this question, I shall begin with a statement on the basis and then discuss it in some detail.

It is generally recognized in the domains of aesthetics and literary criticism that theme is the basis of genre distinction in the literary novel: we know the genre identity of a novel by its theme. Readers of literary novels spontaneously drift toward the genre section of their interest when they desire to read a novel in the library or buy one in the bookstore. They intuitively, and sometimes by practice, know that horror or fantasy novels are found in the horror or fantasy novel section, and they take it for granted that literary novels are classified into genres on the basis of their themes, but they hardly know, and rarely question, the basis, or criterion, of these classifications. They simply expect that the theme of the novels in the horror section will signify horror novels and the theme represented in the romance section will denote romantic novels; most, if not all, of the time, they are not mistaken in their expectation.

However, the question which should pique the interest of the aesthetician and the literary critic is, What do we mean when we say that theme is the basis of genre distinction in a literary novel? I raise this question because a literary novel may contain more than plot, as in Thackery's *Vanity Fair* or *Hardy's Far from the Madding Crowd*, and in fact, many novels contain a multiplicity of themes, some more important than others. For example, a crime novel may contain a passionate love affair and a genuine religious experience. How does one theme acquire precedence or centrality in such novels? In some cases, this precedence is evident, but in others, it is not. Who makes this determination? Can a romantic or a mystery novel be romantic or mysterious to one reader or critic but not to others? Can a novel be romantic in one social or cultural context but not in others? I raise these questions only to emphasize the thesis I discussed in the first section of this paper and plan to explore further in this section, namely, the basis of genre identity inheres in the significant form and emerges as an aesthetic object in the aesthetic experience. Let me elaborate on this argument.

If a novel is a literary work of art, if its literary dimension inheres as a potentiality in its significant form and comes to life as an aesthetic object in the aesthetic experience, that is, if its identity inheres in its structural form, it should follow that *the basis of its genre identity must inhere as a potentiality in its literary dimension*, otherwise, the novel would be voiceless, silent about its identity: it would not be able to declare its identity. All it can say is: "They call me a romantic, mystery, or horror novel." However, suppose a novel is classified as a horror novel, but I experience it as a romantic novel, in other words, suppose the romantic dimension is couched within a theme of horror—would my reading of the novel be correct? Moreover, the assertion that Hardy's novel, *Far from the Madding Crowd*, is a romantic novel logically, and I can add epistemologically, implies that romanticness inheres in it. If, for example, we say that people are rational animals, we certainly imply that rationality is one of their essential, or defining, features. A person who does not instantiate this feature cannot be treated or classified as a rational person. We treat a demented person, one who is insane, as non-rational. Do we not exclude mentally deranged people and children from responsibility on the grounds that they are not in possession of their rational power and consequently cannot distinguish right from wrong or good from bad?

But my critic would ask: if the basis of literary distinction is the formal structure of the novel, what is the basis *of the different genres within the sphere of a literary novel?* Is there one basis? The basis is, as I insisted earlier, theme. Nevertheless, I should immediately add that a basis called "theme" does not exist. What exists is types of themes: romantic, horror, or mystery themes. As a basis of genre distinction, the theme of each genre should inhere as a potentiality in the formal structure of the novel. Accordingly, the quest for a basis of genre distinction in the sphere of the literary novel is in effect a *quest for bases for every genre* within this sphere. If art is the differentiae of literariness, if these differentiae inhere as a potentiality in the novel *qua* significant form, if it comes to life as a world of meaning in the aesthetic experience, then it should follow that, if theme is the basis of a genre distinction in the sphere of literary novel, this theme should define its identity as a particular type of literary novel. If a literary novel is romantic, we should be able to experience its romanticness as its preeminent theme.

My critic would linger on the word "preeminent" and wonder whether a literary novel can have more than one identity, therefore, belonging to more than one genre. I tend to think that a novel can have a multiplicity of themes but one preeminent theme, or identity. Broadly speaking, a novel presents a slice of life. This slice presents a complex amalgamation of individuals, actions, events, scenes, conversations, conflicts, and problems. It is extremely challenging, and sometimes impossible, to depict a theme without necessarily depicting a few or several themes, as is the case in Gabriel G. Marquez' *One Hundred Years of Solitude*. The depiction of such themes does not necessarily detract from the centrality of the major theme of the novel; on the contrary, it supplements and frequently enlivens it. This should not mean that the secondary themes are *secondary* in their value. Although the dominant theme of *The Death of Ivan Ilych* is questioning the meaning of human life, the novel contains several truly significant, and I can add profound, themes. Consider, as an example, Ivan's relationship with Gerasim, the man he treated as an insignificant peasant when he was at the peak of his social and professional success. The focus of this relationship is human love, the kind that originates from an innocent, pure, caring, giving heart and from a mind that intuitively comprehends the laws of nature and serenely abides by their precepts. Who can reflect on this relationship without feeling inspired by the power of true love? But, although secondary, and may be treated as a topic in itself, this theme forms an integral part of the question on the meaning of human life, since love and authenticity represent the foundation of a meaningful life. I think we should view the different themes of a literary novel as an organic unity and its central theme as the principle of this unity. This theme should function as the basis of its genre identity.

Is it possible for critics, or even ordinary readers, to disagree on the central theme of a literary novel? From the standpoint of their theme, some novels are more democratic than others and, the critic might add, some are truly democratic so that it is futile to distinguish a significant theme in some novels. I aver that such disagreements exist and a quick look at the terrain of the literary novel will lend support to this claim, but I think it is quite possible to discover an underlying theme in any democratically weaved novel. Consider Tolstoy's *War and Peace*. This novel presents a panoramic vision of Russian society during a period of destruction, uncertainty, social upheaval, cultural paralysis, social disintegration, political fragility, and moral erosion. This vision embraces several themes, many of which are very significant and may compete for centrality in the novel. Yet, despite this thematic democracy, we glean a general theme, which Tolstoy captures in the title of the novel. Consider, again, *Hardy's Far from the Madding Crowd*. Is the central theme of this novel the power of romantic love—its passion, profundity, patience, and determination—as it is portrayed directly by Gabriel and indirectly by Bathsheba? Is it the tension between romantic and family love? Or, is it the depiction of social life in Southern England in the middle of the nineteenth century? We can read this novel from different points of view or with different bents of mind. The possibility of such difference notwithstanding, we can say that love is the main theme of this novel, and we can argue that Hardy depicted the nature of romantic love in its relation to family love in southern England during the middle of the nineteenth century.

Now we can ask: Is there a method by which we can establish the genre identity of a literary novel? The most realistic and I think the most effective method for establishing this identity is what philosophers call the phenomenological method, according to which we examine the essential elements, or strata, of the novel as they reveal themselves in experiencing it aesthetically (see Ingarden 1973). As I have argued until this point, if a novel is romantic, we should experience it as romantic; accordingly, romanticness must be one of the essential ingredients of the experience. Do we know whether a person is honest by hearsay, how she feels about herself, her social position, the number of degrees she has earned, *or by experiencing her in action*—in how she makes decisions, acts, and conducts herself in the world socially, professionally, religiously, and as a person, particularly in problematic and life-threatening situations? However, the question of determining the genre identity of a literary novel is an empirical one. From an epistemological point of view, we know whether a novel is romantic after we read it, only when we experience its romanticness as one of its essential ingredients. However, the philosopher aims to examine the structure or the features that define the essence of a given reality or reality as a whole. This chapter focuses on the identity of the basis of genre distinction in a literary novel. Does it make a difference whether the author, the literary public, or the critic announces the thematic identity? What matters is whether a literate person can actually experience the thematic identity in the process of reading it. But, is it possible for this reader to be mistaken? Theoretically, yes, and it is possible to read it from a political, ideological, metaphysical, psychological, or religious perspective.

Moreover, it is possible for it to be read differently in different historical periods. Do we read and appreciate the masterpieces of ancient Greek and Roman literature the way people read and appreciated them in those periods? We should always remember that a work of art is an inexhaustible source of meaning and, consequently, of experience. Sometimes the thematic identity of a novel is vague, indeterminate, and resists thematic identification, as we frequently see in Avant Garde, experimental, and post-modern artistic movements. But I am inclined to think that no matter the vagueness, indeterminacy, or elusiveness of its theme, it is possible to distinguish its central theme.

Philosophicalness

Since there are several genres of literary novels, and since one basis of genre identity does not and cannot, in principle, exist, it is incumbent upon aestheticians to articulate the *differentiae* of each genre. Just as we were able to articulate literariness as the defining feature of the literary work of art, we should be able to articulate the feature of each possible genre, for example, horror or romantic novel. In doing this, we should ascertain that this feature inheres as a potentiality in the novel as a significant form and that it comes to life as an essential ingredient of the aesthetic experience (see Goldman 2016; Kuczynska 2018).

In what follows, I shall discuss one literary genre: *the philosophical novel*. I choose this genre only because it is not widely recognized by aestheticians, not to mention the general literary reader. My aim in this discussion is to show in some detail how philosophicalness inheres in the *literary stratum* of the literary novel and how it emerges as a world of meaning in the aesthetic experience. Although philosophical, this world is neither discursive nor descriptive but *a luminous presence*, one we directly see, feel, and comprehend. I shall begin with a brief analysis of the concept of philosophicalness and then discuss how this feature is embodied in the main characters of the novel as metaphors. I shall discuss the concepts of philosophicalness and literariness in greater detail in the following chapters.

What makes a text, a theory, an activity, a discourse, or a question philosophical? An answer to this question should proceed from an adequate understanding of what philosophers actually do—their aims, the domain of their inquiry, and the method they employ to establish the truth or validity of their ideas, theories, or views. *First,* unlike the scientist, whose aim is to explore the essence of the facts that make up the domain of nature, viz., matter, life, and consciousness, the aim of the philosopher is to explore *the meaning of these facts.* While the domain of nature consists of *physical facts,* the domain of meaning consists of *human values*: beauty and its derivatives (e.g., elegance, grandeur, or gracefulness), good and its derivatives (e.g., justice, friendship, or love), truth and its derivatives (e.g., wisdom, erudition, or validity), and metaphysical values (e.g., freedom, purpose, or order). The experience of realizing a particular value is an experience of meaning. The scientist may say that consciousness is reducible to brain processes; the philosopher wonders about the implications of this assertion to moral, religious, social, and artistic life? What does it mean to be free or to pursue ideals in this short life of ours if we are ripples in the cosmic process? How can we understand or explain creativity? How should we live in a world of brute facts? Are human beings evil or good by nature? I will not be too much amiss if I say that the preeminent questions people have been asking since the dawn of human civilization in the areas of morality, art, metaphysics, religion, and culture, constitute the domain of philosophical inquiry.

Second, unlike the scientist who relies exclusively on empirical observation in her endeavor to ascertain the nature of physical facts, the philosopher relies on contemplation. The field of her contemplation is composed of three general dimensions: the mosaic of knowledge articulated by natural and social science, human achievements during the last five millennia in the different areas of civilization and culture, and the philosopher's own observation of the scheme of nature and human life as it unfolds in the course of human history. The aim of this contemplation is to articulate an adequate concept, or understanding, of the world and humanity: Is the world material or spiritual in nature? Why do we exist rather than not? What is the purpose of the universe? Who created it? It is extremely difficult, and I think impossible, to answer the fundamental questions of human life or to explore the nature and validity of human values if we do not proceed in this undertaking from a reasonable understanding of the fabric of human nature—whether our existence and the existence of the world is accidental or purposeful, and if purposeful, who is the source of this purpose. No matter the topic of her inquiry, the vision of the philosopher is always focused on the source, essence, or *arche* of the type of reality she aims to understand.

Third, unlike the scientist who verifies the truth of her claims or theories by way of empirical verification, viz., sensuous observation, instruments, experiments, and mathematical calculation, the philosopher verifies the truth of her claims or theories using logical reasoning conceptual analysis and demonstration. Although the sphere of this method is mind, it is, generally, consistent with the most recent findings of science, established knowledge, and common sense. It would be notoriously odd if the philosopher's claims contradict the testimony of science or common sense, even though this type of contradiction is a frequent occurrence in the history of ideas. However, although the scientist and the philosopher differ in their aims, fields of investigation, and methods of inquiry, they communicate their knowledge discursively. Concept is the medium of communication in both science and philosophy.

However, if philosophical knowledge is essentially discursive, how can a literary novel, which is a work of art, be philosophical? The mere presence of philosophical ideas, questions, problems, or conversations in a novel, no matter their abundance, does not necessarily make it philosophical. If it is philosophical, its philosophical dimension, or character, must be embedded as a potentiality in its literary dimension, but as such a potentiality, it can never be discursive, even though the experience of this dimension may provoke philosophical questions, insights, or ideas in the mind of the person who reads the novel. Thus, the question the philosophical novelist faces is how to transform a content of conceptual meaning into a potential luminous presence, that is, into a meaning we directly intuit as a quality of the situation—event, action, conversation, or problem—we experience in the process of reading the novel aesthetically. How is this possible?

It is critically important to recognize that any symbolic form of expression, philosophic, scientific, or artistic, originates from what a large number of philosophers and artists call *pre-reflective intuition*. This type of intuition is the birthplace of the different types of meaning and consequently any form of symbolic expression—concept, metaphor, image, idea, value, figure of speech, or theory. Do we not call the state of mind, which precedes the formation of a hypothesis, a "hunch?" Does the creative act in any area of human experience, theoretical or practical, not originate from an intuition that emerges from an encounter with a problematic aspect of the universe or from contemplation on the meaning of this or that type of experience? Does the philosopher's system not originate from, and rest on, her fundamental intuition of the nature of the universe as a whole and the meaning of human life? We may view this intuition as "cognitive clay" that can be formed in a multitude of different ways. We should always remember that the realm of inquiry in art and philosophy is the realm of human values: meaning. The mystery that permeates the universe, the purpose of human life, the problems people face in the course of daily living, the basis of happiness, the problem of evil, and the dynamics of human nature—yes, these and related issues which occupy the attention of the philosopher also occupy the attention of the artist.

Let us concede, my critic would now ask, that the intuition and articulation of meaning is the preeminent interest of the philosopher and the artist alike. Essential features of philosophicalness are argument, analysis, and demonstration—does the philosophical novelist argue or demonstrate? No! The philosophical novelist does not argue, analyze, or demonstrate. *She presents; she depicts.* She draws a picture of a moral, metaphysical, religious, social, or political situation *philosophically.* This picture may or may not contain discursive philosophical discourse but instead reveals the life of the values that are implicit in the situation in the fullness of their truth, problematic character, and possibilities. This kind of picture provokes the reader to think about the situation and see its meaning and relevance to the individual and society, creates a moment of self-consciousness and hopefully self-examination, kindles our sense of curiosity, in short, transforms the reader into a momentary philosopher. How can any literate person read *The Death of Ivan Ilych* without having a direct encounter with the ugly face of death, without asking about its significance in her life, without feeling guilty if she discovers that the life she has been leading is a sham? The magic of the literary novel is that it discloses *the world of the possible.* The potential for living in a more profound and wider world of meaning always exists. When we enter this world, we cannot remain speechless; we become "voluntary residents" in it. In the following section, I shall illustrate how philosophicalness inheres in a literary novel and comes to life in the aesthetic experience of the reader. The novel I shall select for analysis is Hermann Hesse's *Narcissus and Goldmund.*

Analysis of a Metaphor

I have so far argued that the literary novel (a) should declare its genre identity from within and (b) the ontological *locus* of this identity is its significant form. This twofold assertion implies that genre identity inheres as a potentiality in the significant form and comes to life as an aesthetic object in the aesthetic experience. The world of this object is a world of meaning. A careful examination of these two propositions will readily show that if a novel is philosophical, its philosophicalness should be an integral part of the aesthetic object; it should shine as the essential quality of the aesthetic experience. How can this quality inhere in the novel as a potentiality in the significant form and become actual in the aesthetic experience?

The proposition I shall now elucidate and defend in this last section of the chapter is that philosophicalness can inhere in the significant form of the novel as a potentiality and become actual in the aesthetic experience *inasmuch* as its main characters and to some extent its scenes and events that are metaphorical in nature (see Beardsley 1981; Putner 2007; Kreitman 2020). Metaphor is an essential artistic category. I shall analyze the concept of metaphor in detail in Chap. 5. However, a few remarks are in order now.

A character can be a metaphor when she stands for a philosophical quality, and she stands for such a quality when she exemplifies it, in what she does, that is, in her action, so that the action reveals the quality. Does Rodin's *The Thinker* not exemplify pictorially the quality of thoughtfulness, usually characteristic of philosophers, in a bronze statue? We intuit this quality directly, by acquaintance, not by a conceptual process. In this context, the character instantiates the essential feature of philosophicalness in the way she speaks, feels, makes decisions, responds to questions and problems, and acts. If, for example, she suddenly finds herself in a problematic situation, she does not respond to it impulsively or emotionally but rationally, reflectively. If the situation involves the value of justice, she reflects on the rule of justice, evaluates the social, psychological, material, and cultural dimensions of the situation, and then translates the essence of the rule into judgment and the judgment into action. This attitude applies to every question or problem she faces in her life. With the wand of creativity in her hand, the novelist translates the essence of the values, beliefs, and questions in the novel into living pictures. Moreover, as a type, the philosophical character always aims at the central values, questions, and problems of human life: happiness, beauty, love, death, hate, justice, freedom, or truth. She always stands as the spokesperson of these values and questions. Is it an accident that all the philosophical novels that punctuate the tapestry of a literary novel struggle with questions and values such as freedom, love, God, faith, and the meaning of human life? One quick look at novels such as *Moby Dick, Remembrance, Of Human Bondage, Middle*

March, Metamorphoses, The Brothers Karamazov, and *The Magic Mountain* will lend credibility to this claim.

Although the philosophical character is an imaginary construct, and although she is essentially a depiction, she acquires a life of her own in the creative hands of the novelist: she becomes a substantial, living reality in the aesthetic experience. We see, feel, and think her the way we see, feel, and think a real person. Indeed, we experience the character as more real than the people we encounter in the streets of social life because we experience her more intimately, more truly, more directly than we experience the ordinary person.

But, my critic would ask, some novels such as Proust's *Remembrance* and Dostoevsky's *The Brothers Karamazov* include philosophical conversations and sometimes arguments—can we still classify them as philosophical novels? Yes. Rational discourse exists in many literary novels. Their presence is secondary, auxiliary, not primary. Their function is to illuminate the meaning of a value, the truth of a belief, or the dynamics of a moral or social problem. They can perform this kind of function only when a philosophical context requires their presence. We should view the prevalence of philosophical thought in a novel like *The Brothers Karamazov* in light of this fact. How can any symbolic form communicate the most difficult questions and values such as evil, God's existence, hate, a lust for power, love, death, or freedom without some appeal to explanation, argument, or conversation? Besides, can we fully comprehend the significance of philosophical thought apart from the literary context in which it is embedded? We think and comprehend it in *The Brothers Karamazov* in terms of this very context: What do people really want? Do they want freedom, true education, a life of Christian love, of beauty, of justice, or alas! of security, a satisfied stomach, and a few crumbs of pleasure, love, freedom, and social recognition? Can we grasp the full significance of these questions, which reach a climax in the Grand Inquisitor scene, *but* within the context of the sudden visit of Jesus to Seville during which he resurrects a child from the dead and then has a chilling, ironic conversation with the Grand Inquisitor? Let me probe the main challenge of this question in some detail by a focused look at Hermann Hesse's *Narcissus and Goldmund.*

Since philosophicalness inheres as a stratum in the literary dimension of the literary novel and since literariness inheres in the novel *qua* significant form, it would be prudent to begin the analysis of *Narcissus and Goldmund* with a synopsis of the novel. I think this is one of Hesse's widely read novels. I shall highlight the parts that are relevant to its literary and philosophical dimensions.

Narcissus and Goldmund is the story of the birth, development, culmination, and glory friendship between two persons who are different emotionally, intellectually, socially, and vocationally but are united by spiritual refinement, good will, and a life guided by the hand of fate. Narcissus is a little older than Goldmund; he is also his teacher both academically and practically. Narcissus is devoted to the life of the mind—to thinking, teaching, truth, and spirituality; Goldmund is devoted to the life of the heart—to feeling, loving, creating, and being. But friendship is either blind or indifferent to age or one's intellectual and affective endowments or vocation; it is the relation between two good human beings. Goodness is its foundation. When their hearts open up to each other, when affection finds its way into the core of their being, this very blindness or indifference is changed into mutual understanding and mutual respect. Difference does not necessarily entail superiority of one to the other; on the contrary, it may create the condition of complementariness between the friends and may in time be a source of mutual enrichment. In his characterization of Narcissus and Goldmund, Hesse writes, "Narcissus was dark and spare; Goldmund a radiant youth. Narcissus was analytical, a thinker; Goldmund, a dreamer with the soul of a child. But something they had in common bridged these contrasts: both were different from the others because of obvious and signs; both bore the special mark of fate" (Hesse, p. 17).

And, indeed, Narcissus the thinker helped Goldmund the dreamer discover himself—his heart, his freedom, his vocation, in short, his destiny. This story begins when Goldmund and his father arrive at Mariabronn Cloister. The purpose of the visit is to enroll Goldmund as a student and when the time is ripe to become a monk. The father, who does not seem to be keenly attached to his son, left Goldmund to the care of Abbot Daniel, and the Abbot left Goldmund to the care of Narcissus as his teacher but not as his confessor. Very soon teacher and student developed a strong feeling of mutual respect and fondness which was transformed into a feeling of mutual affection and shortly afterward into genuine friendship. However, Narcissus was not merely Goldmund's teacher, he also was his mentor, protector, and source of growth and development as a human individual. The life into which Narcissus guided his student was a life freedom, of individuality, of discovery.

Goldmund's first discovery was to recognize the existence of his mother who was for some reason relegated to the world of oblivion. He did not have any knowledge or image of his mother, and yet he missed her. Slowly he realized, and with the help of Narcissus, that the memory of the mother that was hidden within the folds of his inner being stood not only for his real mother but especially for the life of the human heart—of feeling, of motherhood, of femininity, and most of all of the universal mother and giver of life. With this understanding, and the encouraging hand of Narcissus, he began his quest for himself with an enlightening, exciting, and ecstatic adventure with a gypsy woman. This adventure was followed by a life-long string of tender, crushing, elevating, painful, sexual, religious, even criminal adventures. He drank from the infinite ocean of life, and he was drowned in it. The only way he could achieve his goal as a dreamer was to be a vagrant, a wanderer, and a gypsy. He lived as a free person. He listened to the voice of his heart and mind and to no other voice. He was a vivid embodiment of the free spirit of Dionysius. He was an explosion of life, a life in search of itself—of meaning, of understanding, of love, of beauty, of God, and of being. In fact, he found himself, and the self he found was the self of an artist. This find was one of the most delicious fruits of his life of wandering. The spirit of the creative mother in him burst into an artist under the guidance of a highly respected artist: Master Niklaus. His works exhibited profound aesthetic beauty. This final development, which produced in his mind a sense of fulfillment, prompted him to return to Narcissus, his friend. Narcissus welcomed him with open arms, and the arms that welcomed him were caring, loving, tender, supportive, and constructive.

Read as a story, *Narcissus and Goldmund* is not a literary work of art; consequently it is not a philosophical novel. It is mainly a tale about a young man, Goldmund, who was abandoned first by his mother and then by his father. He was placed in a cloister with the expectation that he will become a monk. But when he approaches the end of his adolescence he leaves the cloister and becomes a wanderer, a vagrant. His life consists of a series of sexual conquests, murders, and social blunders during which he was exposed to death several times. But read as a literary work, this novel is a fascinating *depiction* of the essence, life, glory, and value of true friendship. Now we can ask: What makes *Narcissus and Goldmund* a philosophical novel?

We can say, as I shall argue later, that it is philosophical because philosophy is its preeminent theme. This claim is based on the assumption that theme is the principle of genre distinction. But this novel does not have only one but several philosophical themes: transience, happiness, freedom, art, friendship, and God. Although Narcissus and Goldmund converse on these and other themes conceptually only as a way of expressing certain feelings or ideas about them, the novel is not philosophical because of these conversations but because the themes they converse about are communicated *depictively*. That is, although the main characters express their feelings or views on the nature of friendship, transience, freedom, God, or happiness conceptually, only as a part of the unfolding thread of the plot, they do not explain, argue, clarify, justify, analyze, or verify the truth or falsity of any of the ideas they converse about. Put differently, they do not act as philosophers; they do not try to communicate their ideas or views philosophically but by the way they live or act. The basic structure of the novel is action, and their action discloses its philosophical theme. Philosophicalness exists in the medium of this action as a luminous presence. We directly see, intuit, this quality in the action. We do not discern it or apprehend it by the philosophical activity of explaining, arguing, justifying, or clarifying any of the ideas the characters converse about.

But a critic would now ask: "How does the thread that makes up the structure of the novel depict its philosophical theme?" My critic raises this question because the theme of *Narcissus and Goldmund* revolves around several philosophical concepts. Can a multiplicity of philosophical concepts be depicted in a literary novel? My answer to the second question is yes because like all literary novels, *Narcissus and Goldmund* is a slice of human life. Such a slice is a microcosm that necessarily expresses or raises some of the fundamental questions philosophers have been trying to answer for more than two millennia. What matters in the present context is the extent to which the philosophical content of the novel is articulated and communicated depictively. Frequently, one philosophical question either implies or is logically related to other questions. For example, can we discuss the question of friendship without some encounter with the question of freedom, happiness, or the different moral values? The challenge we face in our attempt to explain the philosophicalness of a literary novel is not whether it contains one or more philosophical question or idea but whether these questions or ideas exist in the novel *in the mode of depiction*. The proposition I shall now elucidate is that the central theme of *Narcissus and Goldmund* is friendship and that the other philosophical questions are directly or indirectly implicated by this theme. This assertion is evident in the title of the novel as well as in the development of its plot. The novel begins with the encounter that joined Narcissus and Goldmund in the bond of friendship and ends with the glorious triumph of this very friendship.

It is critically important to recognize that the conception, or understanding of true friendship, Hesse depicts in *Narcissus and Goldmund* is essentially Aristotle's conception which we find in the *Nichomachean Ethics*. This conception has remained the paradigm and the basic source of insight in any discourse about friendship during the past 2500 years. Now, how does Narcissus and Goldmund embody this conception? But first, what are defining elements of Aristotle's conception of true friendship? How can we say that a certain character embodies the essential nature of true friendship if we do not know the kind of friendship the characters embody? As a reminder, I shall outline its basic elements.

For Aristotle, true friendship is, *first*, a bond of affection, or love, between two human beings. This bond consists of mutual attraction, the kind that originates from the heart, mind, and will of the friends. *Second*, the basis of this bond is goodness in two basic ways: the friends are attracted to each other because they are good and because they aim at the good in their personal life and the life of the community in which they thrive. *Third*, this bond is not abstract but concrete. It is established and promoted by sharing their ideas, feelings, desire, experiences, and hopes for the future. The more they share, the more they know each other, and the more they share and know each other, the greater is their mutual love. *Fourth*, true friends treat each other as equals. No one treats oneself or the other as superior or inferior. Their equality is an equality of goodness, of good will. They may differ in what they do or achieve, but they do not differ in the way or magnitude of their love for each other. *Fifth*, true friends assume a constructive, productive attitude toward each other. This means they do not blame, reprimand, or punish each other; on the contrary, they are naturally inclined to heal, help, and enable each other to grow and be better human beings. *Sixth*, because the basis of their friendship is goodness, and because goodness is lasting, true friendship is lasting.

It is important to emphasize at the outset that when I say that a character embodies a certain conception of friendship, I assume, as I shall discuss in detail in Chap. 5, that the character functions in the novel as a metaphor, and, as a character, he or she exemplifies in her behavior the essential meaning of the signification of the metaphor, in the present case, Aristotle's conception of truer friendship. I say "essential" only because the kind of meaning it embodies is a possibility for indeterminate and varied realizations. It is now appropriate to explain, more pointedly, how *Narcissus and Goldmund* depicts the essential nature of true friendship.

Please, dear reader, focus your critical, analytical attention on the first scene of the novel in which Goldmund arrives at Mariabronn Cloister. In this scene, we do not find a philosophical or any other kind of intellectual discourse between Narcissus and Goldmund on the nature of friendship, much less on Aristotle's conception of moral virtue. We simply witness an encounter between two human beings, one older than the other. During this encounter, in which Narcissus, the critical and analytical mind, has an occasion to discern a vibrant, innocent, intelligent, lovable, restless soul, a soul that has not yet met the world or even knows what human life is about but, nevertheless, a soul that is ripe and willing to explore both the world and the meaning of human life. Narcissus welcomes him as his student and in fact he is happy to have such a student. It does not take Goldmund long to respond positively to the high-minded Narcissus, to admire him, to be his student, and most of all to feel a strong affection for him. This type of reaction could not have emerged had he not felt the affection that exuded from Narcissus' soul during this encounter. Hesse did not give us a discourse about the nature of this affection; he simply depicted the circumstance under which it was felt by both characters. And indeed, we discover, when Goldmund is still a novice at the cloister, that they existentially recognized their mutual affection and referred to each other as friends. Although he performed his role as a teacher competently and effectively, Narcissus also performed his role as a friend competently and effectively. The first objective he pursued was *to help Goldmund discover himself and to be himself.* Can such an objective be conceived and realized but from a *good will?* As teachers and psychologists know quite well, this is a formidable challenge. It is as formidable as the challenge Michaelangelo faced when he carved *David* out of that famous slab of marble or Phidias faced when he carved *Lemnian Athena* out of a similar slab of marble. This is the kind of challenge Narcissus faced when his affection for Goldmund exploded in his heart, when the bond of friendship between them was deep and true.

But although Narcissus was older than Goldmund and was his teacher, he never acted or treated Goldmund as his inferior but always as his equal as a human being and as a friend. We discover this aspect early on in their relationship as friends. As I pointed out earlier, Narcissus and Goldmund are different from each other as types of character, for they are endowed with different emotional, intellectual, social, and vocational endowments. This necessarily implies that they may be superior to each other in certain types of behavior or achievements but not as friends and certainly not as human individuals. Hesse did not discuss this dimension of their friendship; he let his characters reveal it in one of their conversations, which is a mode of action, when Goldmund remarked that Narcissus was superior to him: "Why, yes," Narcissus continued, "Natures of your kind, with strong, delicate senses, the soul-oriented, the dreamers, poets, lovers are almost always superior to us creatures of the mind. You take your being from your mother. You live fully; you were endowed with the strength of love, the ability to feel. Whereas we creatures of reason, we don't live fully; we live in an arid land, even though we often seem to guide and rule you. Yours is the plentitude of life, the sap of the fruit, the garden of passion, the beautiful landscape of art. Your home is the earth; ours is the world of ideas. You are in danger of drowning in the world of the senses; ours is the danger of suffocating in an airless world. You are an artist; I am a thinker. You sleep at the mother's breast; I wake in the desert. For me the sun shines; for you the moon and stars" (Hesse 1968, p. 45).

This response spotlights goodness and equality as essential features of true friendship. It may seem at first that Narcissus is the giver of goodness, for he is the teacher, the guiding vision, and the driving force of Goldmund's life, while Goldmund is merely the receiver of this goodness, but in fact it is not the case. How can a young man, a man who has not become a productive citizen of the world, give to his teacher except his love? But Goldmund began to give and to objectify his love for Narcissus the moment he flowered as a human individual, and the first flower of his creation was a life-size statue of Narcissus which he baptized as St. John. Was the flowering of this artist not the handiwork of Narcissus' love for him? Can we ignore the dramatic omnipresence of Narcissus in Goldmund's consciousness in the major adventures he had when he was sick, when he committed murders, when he suffered the harshness of the plague, or when he spent many a lonely night in the cold weather or in the forests?

Consider, next, the purity of the bond of affection between the two friends. Their friendship was not based on pleasure or advantage. The quid pro quo principle was banned from their consciousness. Did Narcissus not accept Goldmund for his own sake, for the innocence and goodness that shone from him in all his action? For example, did he change or complain when Goldmund left for so many years or when Goldmund gave him a report about his adventures and mis-adventures? Did Narcissus express any feeling of anger, lament, or sorrow, or disappointment when he knew of these and similar adventures? Although Goldmund changed, although he aged, Narcissus never reprimanded, admonished, or in any way complained about any of his friend's actions. The glittering jewel of goodness that radiated in his friend's heart remained the source of his love for him to the end. What was that kiss he pressed on Goldmund's lips after Goldmund surrendered his soul to the world of non-being but an expression of the fire of love for each other?

But goodness is, moreover, lasting. Does the glittering jewel that sits on the throne of the human heart lose its sheen, fade, or change? Was Narcissus not the center of Goldmund's life and always gravitated toward this center? Was Goldmund not the sole inhabitant of Narcissus' heart? Did he not spontaneously cry, when Goldmund returned to him, Thank God you returned to me? Unlike advantage or pleasure, which are transient, since they are parts of the natural process, goodness is an integral part of the world of the spirit. This world resists change; it abides in the human heart.

When I read *Narcissus and Goldmund* I do not read a philosophy discourse about friendship. I read the story of a life of friendship. The story I read is a picture, a delineation, a living presence of this life. I witness its dynamics and I comprehend them in the fullness of their being. I comprehend the bone and flesh of friendship as a value and as a concrete, living relation between two human beings who are completely different from each other in terms of their social, emotional, vocational, and intellectual endowments but completely alike in their good will, in their human refinement, vision, and capacities.

Concluding Remark

I began this chapter with an inquiry into the nature of the basis of genre in a literary novel. It is generally recognized that theme is the basis of genre distinction within this sphere. But, as I pointed out, it is not clear how theme exists in the novel and how it functions as a principle of genre distinction: What is the ontological locus of theme in a literary novel? How does it emerge in the aesthetic experience? I focused my attention on this question because if, for example, a novel is romantic, it must declare its romantic identity. This claim is based on the assumption that it cannot make this declaration if the basis of its identity does not inhere in it. How does it inhere in it? In the preceding pages, I elucidated and defended the thesis that the theme of the literary novel inheres in its literary dimension and that this dimension, in turn, inheres in the novel as a significant form. Possession of aesthetic qualities is what makes a novel a literary work of art. Theme exists as a potentiality in the medium of the aesthetic dimension of the literary novel and emerges as an aesthetic object during the aesthetic experience. In *The Philosopher and the Devil*, it exists as a metaphor. The aesthetic object unfolds in the aesthetic experience as *a world of meaning*. Any reference to or discourse about the theme of a literary novel, critical or analytical, is a reference to or a discourse about this world. It should *be the basis of literary appreciation and criticism in a literary novel*. In a philosophical novel, the characters as well as the events, which make up the thread of its plot, are metaphors. In this and similar cases, metaphor, or any other type of symbolic form, is the building block of the aesthetic stratum of the literary novel.

References and Suggested Bibliography

Bailey, John (1975). *Tolstoy and the Novel*. London: Macmillan.
Beardsley, Monroe (1981). Aesthetics. Indianapolis: Hackett Publishing.
Bell, Clive (1958). *Art*. New York: Capricorn Books.
Cassirer, Ernst (1962). *An Esay on Man*. New Haven: Yale University Press.
Dufrenne, Mikel (1973). *Phenomenology of Aesthetic Experience*. Evanston: Northwestern University Press.
Goldman, Alan H. (2016). *Philosophy and the Novel*. Oxford: Oxford University Press.
Hesse, Hermann (1968). *Narcissus and Goldmund*. New York: Picador.
Ingarden, Roman (1973). *The Literary Work of Art, Evanston*. Iniana: Northwestern University Press.
Kreitman, Norman (2020). *The Roots of Metaphor: A Multidisciplinary Study in Aesthetics*. Routledge.
Kuczynska, Alicja (2018). *Art as a Philosophy*, in *Dialogue and Universalism*, issue 28; (1988); "Qualities of Things and Aesthetic qualities," in Mitias (1988), *Aesthetic Quality and Aesthetic Experience*.
Langer, Susan. (1951). *Philosophy in a New Key*. Cambridge: Harvard University Press.
Mitias, Michael. (1987). *What Makes an Experience Aesthetic?* Rodopi; *The Possibility of Aesthetic Experience*. Amsterdam: *Kluwer, 1987*; *Aesthetic Quality and Aesthetic Experience*. Amsterdam: Rodopi, 1988; *The Philosopher and the Devil*, London: Olympia, 2018.
Porter, Burton (2004). *Philosophy Through Fiction and Film*. Upper Sadler River: Pearson Prentice-Hall.
Putner, David (2007). *Metaphor*. New York: Routledge.

CHAPTER 3

The Philosophical Novel as a Literary Genre

INTRODUCTION

The proposition I shall elucidate and defend in this chapter is that, as a literary work of art, the philosophical novel should be treated as a genre; accordingly, it should stand on par with genres such as romantic, adventure, mystery, or picaresque novels, primarily because it has the basic elements and features which make it a *type*. As a genre, the philosophical novel is distinguished as a novel genre by its theme. The central focus of this theme is a philosophical question, issue, insight, idea, value, or problem. In this context, theme functions as a *principium individionis*—that is, as a criterion on the basis of which we distinguish a certain type as a genre. We cannot underestimate the importance of this criterion, as the theme the novelist chooses for her novel determines, to a large extent, its essential character, or type. This theme functions as a basis for *organizing* the plot; it is, moreover, the source of its unity and the type of qualities that emerge in the experience of the novel as a literary work of art.

Let us grant for the sake of discussion that the philosophical novel is a type by virtue of its theme; how does it contain and communicate its philosophical content? That is, how does this content reach the reader? Again, what kind of experience does the reader have of the philosophical novel? If the novel is philosophical, its experience should also be philosophical—so what makes this experience philosophical? I raise these questions for three main reasons. First, the *mere presence* of philosophical

© The Author(s), under exclusive license to Springer Nature Switzerland AG 2022
M. H. Mitias, *The Philosophical Novel as a Literary Genre*,
https://doi.org/10.1007/978-3-030-97385-8_3

content as a dominant theme, in the form of a discursive text, conversation, or analysis, in a novel does not, as discussed earlier, necessarily make it philosophical; on the contrary, this kind of presence may deprive it of its literary core because the literary work of art is an expressive, not a discursive work. But if the novel is a literary work, it should express its philosophical identity the way a work of art does. The philosophical content should be an ingredient of its literary being. A novel can be literary without necessarily being philosophical, but a philosophical novel cannot be philosophical without being literature. As philosophy, the novel's philosophical content is only the *differentiae* of the novel *qua* literature. I experience the romantic character of a romantic novel not because a character pronounces a statement such as "I love you," because she expounds a theory of love or because she praises its benefits but in and through the action the lovers perform—that is, in and through the totality of the actions that make up the thread of the novel. We should make a distinction between thinking the idea of love and experiencing it as a mode of meaning in a concrete situation or behavior.

Second, if we say that the mere presence of philosophical content as a dominant theme in a novel is what makes it philosophical, we necessarily undercut the possibility of having an aesthetic, or literary, experience of it. A novel is, as I shall explain in detail later, a literary work of art inasmuch as it possesses aesthetic qualities. The unity of these qualities is what is generally recognized by aestheticians as the "aesthetic object" (see, e.g., Mitias 1987; Dufrenne 1973; Ingarden 1973). These qualities are the reason for being of the novel as a literary work of art. We do not read a literary novel simply because it is an interesting story; because it is a source of psychological, scientific, or historical knowledge; or because we need to kill some time (although we can certainly read it for such purposes), but in order to have an aesthetic experience of it. As a literary work, the novel comes to life in the process of reading it; its aesthetic dimension emerges through this process. This dimension is not, as I shall explain, given as a ready-made reality; it is creatively constructed in the activity of reading the novel aesthetically. However, saying that the mere presence of some philosophical content in it is what makes a novel philosophical is tantamount to saying that its literary dimension is given as a ready-made reality. Yet, as I have just pointed out, the literary dimension of the novel is not given as a ready-made reality but as a potentiality for realization in the aesthetic experience. The point which deserves special emphasis here is that if we say that the mere presence of philosophical content is what makes the novel philosophical, we reduce the experience to a purely philosophical one—but the novel is a literary, not a philosophical, work.

Third, the presence of philosophical content in a novel may enrich it aesthetically, intellectually, and in some other respects, but this kind of presence does not necessarily make it philosophical. A large number of major literary novels in the western tradition raise significant philosophical questions, include illuminating philosophical conversations, and enhance our awareness of the importance of philosophical reflection in certain situations in our lives, but hardly any serious critic would view them as philosophical novels. Similarly, the mere presence of religious, scientific, or political content in a novel does not necessarily make the book religious, scientific, or political in character, even though such content may exist as a basic ingredient in the work.

As an aspect, "philosophicalness" cannot be reduced to the mere presence of some philosophical content in a literary novel but should be treated as a feature that permeates and shines through the work as an organic unitary quality in the process of reading it aesthetically. The locus of philosophicalness is the literary experience. The aesthetic, as such, is the aim of the artist in the process of creating the artwork and of the reader in the process of reading the novel aesthetically. Accordingly, we should make a distinction between (1) philosophicalness that emerges in the aesthetic experience and (2) the mere presence of a certain philosophical content in a work. The first is the essential aesthetic quality of the work, one that permeates and shines through the totality of the aesthetic object in the aesthetic experience; the second is a conceptual, discursive content. The first *emerges* in the course of the aesthetic experience; the second is *given* as an ingredient in the structure of the novel as a story. The first is received by the intellect, while the second is apprehended by the imagination; the first is thought in the medium of concepts, while the second is intuited in the medium of feeling. Thus, a philosophical novel may or may not contain discursively given philosophical content. In some cases, the presence of such content may enhance the depth and power of the novel, while in others it may detract from this. This is based on the assumption that the explication, illumination, and elucidation of the philosophical, as such, are not restricted to the articulation and communication of concepts but extend to the different forms of symbolic or artistic expression.

But what is philosophicalness, or the philosophical? Under what conditions can a literary novel be classified as a philosophical type, or as genre? I aver that an answer to this question is not easy to give because philosophers have frequently differed on the aims, nature, and method of philosophy. I do not exaggerate in saying that the history of philosophy from its inception to the present, especially during the nineteenth and twentieth centuries, is an amazing mosaic of complexity, diversity, disagreements, conflicts, and kaleidoscopic views and achievements. And yet, in spite of this colorful mosaic, philosophers view themselves as philosophers and their work as philosophical. What makes their work philosophical?

As I shall presently explain, an answer to this question is an indispensable condition for an adequate understanding of what makes a philosophical novel as a genre. A second indispensable condition is an adequate analysis of the aspect that makes a novel a literary work of art, primarily because the locus of philosophicalness is its literariness. Accordingly, an adequate analysis of what makes a novel literary and what makes an idea, text, or question philosophical—and, consequently, what makes a literary novel philosophical—will provide a reasonable answer to the question of why we should treat the philosophical novel as a genre.

Philosophicalness

What makes an activity or a proposition philosophical? Like the scientist, the philosopher is a seeker of knowledge. Well, what sort of object, or types of reality, does she endeavor to know? If the realm of nature is the object of scientific inquiry, what is the realm of philosophical inquiry? Does anything exist besides, or other than, the realm of nature? Yes! Philosophers are not in agreement on the identity of the aim and object of philosophical inquiry, but I believe that, with a few exceptions such as materialism and some schools of analytic philosophy, the majority of philosophers would say that the realm of philosophical inquiry is the realm of *human values or meaning*. The scientist seeks to know the objects which make up the scheme of nature; the philosopher seeks to know the *meaning* of these objects. The realm of human values is the realm of meaning; meaning is realized value. When we say that something is valuable, we mean that it is meaningful; we also mean that the experience of that something is meaningful: satisfying or satisfactory. Moreover, the philosopher seeks to know the meaning that underlies the existence of the universe, including the meaning of human life and destiny.

When I speak of human values, I mean, first, *truth* and its derivatives in science, philosophy, religion, history, economics, government, and the other disciplines of knowledge; second, *beauty* in nature, human beings, and art and its derivatives such as splendor, grandeur, elegance, tragedy, comedy, joy, and horror; third, *goodness* and its derivatives such as love, generosity, courage, justice, and honesty. We treat truth, beauty, and goodness as values not merely because people desire them, for they may desire them selfishly or expediently, but because they are *essential needs*, because they are indispensable to *human being*: we cannot be the human beings we are, and should be, if we do not meet these needs. Some philosophers have characterized these qualities as intrinsic, in the sense that they are valuable in themselves, because we seek them for their own sake, because their value inheres in them and nowhere else, but I tend to think that they acquire this aspect primarily because they are responses to essential needs inherent in human nature.

Values do not fall from heaven; they are human creations. Neither the philosopher, the theologian, nor the politician legislates values, although each may play a significant role in clarifying their meaning, interpreting them, or examining the existential conditions under which they can be realized in the lives of human beings. They originate from the bosom of human experience in the course of social and cultural progress. However, inasmuch as they are human creations, they exist as ideals, and as ideals, they are *schemas*, general plans for particular actions and types of action. They grow in their meaning, depth, and richness. Their growth is always a response to the growth of human needs. The task of the philosopher is to know their nature and limits and the extent to which they can be realized in the life of a given society.

Now, if the object of study in philosophy is the realm of human values, what method should the philosopher employ in their study? It would seem that, because this realm is not made up of physical facts, sensory observation cannot, at least not directly, be used in the study of this realm. I say "not directly" for two reasons: first, because their study is impossible without an understanding of the structure and dynamics of human nature, and second, because the field in which human nature is studied is the history of human civilization. Accordingly, although the realm of values is generically different from the realm of nature, and therefore cannot be reduced to material terms, it cannot be studied apart from an understanding of the material conditions of human life.

Let us grant that the realm of values is generically different from the realm of nature, my critic might now ask: What makes an activity, an idea, or a theory of value philosophical? An answer to this question should begin with an analysis of the method the philosopher employs in her study of this realm. What is this method? But first, what is the *ontological status* of human values or what is their *mode of existence*? We cannot inquire into the nature of any object if we do not know where and how it exists. For example, the chair on which I am now sitting is a physical object. I can point to it and I or any other person can identify it in a certain way primarily because it exists in a particular space during a stretch of time. In other words, we know this chair exists by sensory observation. This type of observation is the basis of its identification as a particular object. Let us now ask, what is the mode of existence of a value such as justice? We can readily say that it is not a part of the furniture of the natural realm. We see people walking in the street and trees growing in the garden, but we do not see justice walking in the street or growing in the garden! Yet if it is not a part of the realm of nature, it should be a part of the world of the human mind. As such, it exists as an idea; and as a type of idea, it exists as an *ideal;* and as an ideal, it exists, as I have just indicated, as a *schema* or a plan of action—that is, it exists as a possibility for realization as a type of action, whether individually or socially. However, although this type of ideal exists in the mind, it does not exist as a purely subjective, idiosyncratic, or fictitious reality but as a general, intersubjective, communicable, and objectively verifiable reality.

Now, by what method does the philosopher study this and similar values? What is involved in this study? This method consists of three basic elements: analysis, evaluation, and argument or demonstration. Regardless of whether it is a metaphysical, moral, aesthetic, religious, or political proposition; a theory; or a point of view in any sphere of human values, the philosopher employs these three intellectual tools in the study of the nature and conditions under which a value can be realized in action. Let us, for example, ask: What is the nature of justice? In answering this question, the philosopher proceeds from the assumptions that (1) this value originates as a response to an essential need in human nature and (2) it cannot be understood apart from the way it is applied in the course of the history of human civilization. Thus, in studying this value, the philosopher reflects on the dynamics of this need and the way it is understood and applied by the different societies of the world. Like the scientist, the philosopher's aim is to establish the truth of a certain proposition or theory on the nature of a value such as friendship; and like the scientist, who focuses her attention on the essence of the object of knowledge, the philosopher focuses her attention on the essence of a certain value. However, unlike the realm of nature, which is given as a ready-made reality, the realm of values is not given as a ready-made reality but as a potentiality, as a reality in continual need of interpretation and conceptual articulation—not only because the meaning of values changes from one society to another but also because it changes within the same society from one historical period to another. This is why the study of the realm of values is to some extent problematic. We encounter this feature in the different philosophical disciplines: metaphysics, which examines the meaning of the universe; ethics, which examines the meaning of happiness; aesthetics, which examines the meaning of beauty; political philosophy, which examines the meaning of justice; and so forth. This feature is inherent in the structure of value primarily because it is a *schema*—that is, a potentiality for infinite possible realizations. It is extremely difficult for the philosopher to capture or articulate the spectrum of these possibilities in one interpretation or grasp. Understanding the nature of a value always depends on developing an understanding of the continual growth and development of the different sciences, arts, technologies, and cosmologies, as well as the newly emerging cultural, educational, economic, and social conditions of society. Penetrating the structure of this spectrum is an unusually intricate, deep, and vast undertaking. It increases in its intricacy, depth, and vastness particularly because values are enmeshed in individual and social situations and because they frequently conflict with each other. Consider the value of love. Can you imagine the infinite types and ways of loving human beings at the individual and institutional levels? Can you imagine the multitude of theories, definitions, and interpretations of this value by philosophers, social scientists, and theologians? Consider, too, the value of justice. Can you imagine all the definitions, treatises, and legal and ethical codes of justice created by philosophers and legislators? Finally, consider Plato's attempt to define this value in the *Republic* and how, soon after completing the first chapter, he found it necessary to discuss other values in education, ethics, epistemology, metaphysics, art, god, immortality, and related questions! The greatness of a philosophical work lies in its capacity to disclose the wealth of the possible realizations that are hidden in the womb of value as a potentiality.

And yet, despite the indeterminacy, intricacy, fluidity, and problematic character of values, one of the essential features which distinguishes philosophical thought as a type of knowledge and method is insight. The philosopher may not be able to produce finally tested propositions in some cases, but she can, in and through her theories, communicate insight or a glimmer of understanding into the nature of a given value. Philosophy can, at least, show a value's complexity and suggest ways of discovering the conditions under which it can be understood or realized. No one metaphysical, ethical, aesthetic, or political theory or view contains a final answer to the question of the meaning of the universe, of human life, of beauty, or of the good society, but each certainly contains a wealth of understanding of these and other types of value questions.

However, the question which interests the philosopher is not how a certain conception of a value such as justice comes into being in this or that society or culture, although such an inquiry is vitally important to her study, but what conception is the most appropriate response to the essential need for justice. An adequate conception should take into consideration the dynamics of this need and the logical conditions under which it can be understood and realized, given certain social, political, cultural, educational, and technological conditions. In arriving at such a conception, the philosopher relies on two basic types of knowledge. The first comes from natural science, for example, physics, biology, and chemistry; the second comes from social sciences, for example, psychology, sociology, economics, and history. Reflecting on these two types of knowledge is the ultimate source of the philosopher's interpretation or view of the nature of human values. For example, the metaphysician always advances her view of the ultimate meaning or purpose of the universe on the basis of the most recent theories in physics, geology, and cosmology; the ethicist advances her view of the good life on the basis of the most recent theories of human nature in the social sciences; the aesthetician advances her view of the nature of art on the basis of the most recent developments in mathematics, physics, zoology, linguistics, and technology. Clearly, it is difficult for the philosopher to examine the nature of values without a genuine grasp of the significance and implications of the most recent discoveries in the different sciences.

As we can see, the basis of philosophical reflection on the nature of values is knowledge, and the aim of this reflection is also knowledge. The first type of knowledge, which comes from the sciences, is founded in sensory observation. This type of observation is the source of this knowledge and the basis of its verification. This aspect is why we can say that *the sensory* is the stuff of scientific-ness. However, philosophical knowledge is founded in *thought*; it is derived from reflection, specifically reflection on the different types of scientific knowledge, and it is verified by a rigorous methodology involving logical analysis, evaluation, and argumentation. This is why we can reasonably say that thought is the stuff of philosophicalness, and the aim of this thought is to understand, to be enlightened, to have insight. Like the scientist who aims at the essence of material objects and verifies the validity of her knowledge in the medium of sensory observation, the philosopher aims at the essence of values and verifies the validity of her knowledge in the medium of thought. The method of arriving at knowledge in both areas determines the nature of the kind of thinking done in them.

LITERARINESS

A "novel" is a "story," but not every story is a novel. I am quite aware that a large number of people, including some art critics, frequently use the two terms interchangeably. It is not my purpose here to question or criticize this practice. I simply wish to emphasize that by "novel," I mean a literary work of art which stands on par with the major artistic forms. Like every art form, the novel is differentiated by virtue of its medium, viz., the word. Unlike painting, whose medium is lines and colors; music, whose medium is sound; or dance, whose medium is motion, the medium of literature comprises a certain type of *linguistic structure*, for example, prose or poetry. But literature is a vast and diverse artistic domain. It embraces arts such as drama, biography, poetry, or novel. Each of these art forms is viewed as a class or genre. For example, poetry includes genres such as epic, pastoral, heroic, or lyric poetry; the novel includes genres such as mystery, romantic, fantasy, or adventure fiction. A general survey of the different types of literary novel will show that the "philosophical novel" is not treated by the majority of critics as a genre. The main thesis of this paper, as stated earlier, is that it should be treated as a genre. This proposition implies that the philosophical novel is (1) a *literary* work of art and (2) a *philosophical* work of art. The line of reasoning that underlies my thesis is that if the philosophical novel is a literary work of art—if it is philosophical the way a romantic or a mystery novel are romantic and mystery novels—it should follow that if a novel is literary and philosophical—that is, if philosophicalness is its defining characteristic as a literary work of art—then it should be treated as a genre. In what follows, I shall elucidate and defend the claim that a novel can be philosophical and that if it can be philosophical, it should be classified as a genre. In discussing this thesis, I shall focus my attention on two questions: What makes a novel a literary work of art? What makes a novel *qua* art philosophical? I shall discuss the first question in this section and the second in the following section.

What Makes a Novel a Literary Work of Art?

My quest in raising this question is a quest for literariness—the aspect, or factor, whose presence in a novel makes it a literary work of art. This aspect, I submit, is *art*, or *artistic-ness*—the aspect whose presence in any artifact makes, or transforms, it into a work of art. A novel is a literary work of art inasmuch as it is *art*. Accordingly, a novel is an anecdote or an account of a series of happenings or events that revolve around a theme. The theme can be love, war, hate, justice, faith, or any interesting subject. When I read a story, I wish to know what happens, always what happens, next. My interest in the story focuses on the plot as the vehicle that underlies the development of the theme, on the extent to which it is pleasant, appealing, exciting, or dramatic. The basis of this interest is the kind of plot the author has woven in the process of writing the story. The plot is, moreover, the basis of my evaluation of its beauty, mediocrity, or ugliness.

But the novel is more than a story; on the contrary, the plot is only its vehicle or backbone. Its identity as a novel is qualitatively different from its identity as a story. What is this quality, or identity? To my mind, it is the same identity which makes any artifact an artwork. This is based on the generally recognized assumption that in literature, the art-making aspect is the literary-making aspect. What is this art-making aspect?

The principle of *artistic distinction* is possession of *aesthetic qualities:* an artifact is art inasmuch as it possesses aesthetic qualities. These qualities do not exist in the work as ready-made qualities, or as sensory or conceptual realities, the way sentences, scenes, actions, or characters are given but as potentialities inherent in its form. By "aesthetic qualities" I mean qualities such as enigma, mystery, irony, horror, sadness, joy, terror, comedy, tragedy, splendor, or grandeur. They *emerge* in the aesthetic experience and they do not exist outside this experience. Their unity in the given artwork constitutes what I shall call "significant form." The presence of this form in the work is what makes it *art* and its realization in the experience of the work is what makes the experience *aesthetic.* Consequently, its presence in a novel is what makes it a literary work of art, and its presence in the experience is what makes it a literary or aesthetic experience. The point I should stress here is that "the aesthetic" is the defining character of "the literary." Now, let me explain and defend this thesis in some detail.

Like the table, the car, or the telephone, the artwork is an artifact—a purposefully made object. However, not every artifact is an artwork. For example, the chair on which I am now sitting is an artifact, but it is not an artwork, although it may be considered one if an artist like Marcel Duchamp were to place it in a museum under conditions specified by what is generally known as "the art world." Accordingly, we should ask: What makes an object an artwork?

Broadly speaking, we can say that possession of aesthetic qualities by an artifact is what makes it an artwork. The unity of these qualities, which is produced by the artist—for example, Vermeer's *Kitchen Maid*, which hangs on the wall in a museum, or a performance of Sophocles' *Oedipus the King* in a theater—is called "significant form" by a large number of aestheticians (see Bell 1958; Dufrenne 1973; Mitias 1987). In the artistic process, the artist does not create her medium; rather, she uses it in the creation of the work—she forms it in a certain way. Put differently, she imposes a certain form on it. The form she creates is *significant* inasmuch as it is a *meaningful* form. But what about this type of form that makes it meaningful? If I am to answer this question in one word, I can say *importance*. "Importance" is a basic category; it denotes a primordial experience of something that matters to us. We usually refer to this quality by the term "value." Any object, event, or relation is valuable insofar as it is important—that is, inasmuch as it is significant, worthwhile, or meaningful. The concept of importance is not defined in terms of other concepts but in terms of the basic features of the kind of experience it creates.

The experience of aesthetic qualities in an artwork, a natural object, or a human being is what makes it meaningful. We deem the aesthetic as such valuable, and we appreciate an object that possesses such qualities mainly because its experience is meaningful or valuable. The concept of meaning is a correlate to the concept of value because, ontologically speaking, the experience of meaning is always an experience of realized value. For example, a piece of music is an organization of sounds, but not every organization of sounds is necessarily music. Ordinary speech is an organization of sounds and so is the wind, but neither is music, even though many people enjoy the sound of the wind or of a particular spoken language. However, when sounds are organized, that is, formed, in a certain way so as to produce a *Vales Triste* the way Sibelius did, it becomes music. This type of organization, which is a type of language, acts on us in a certain way, so that when we listen to it aesthetically, we feel the sadness it embodies as a quality inherent in that specific organization of sounds.

I characterize a musical form as a kind of language primarily because it is a purposeful organization of sounds, and it is purposeful because it embodies and communicates a certain type of meaning. Every purpose we pursue signifies a value, and every value we realize is a realization of meaning. The type of meaning we enjoy depends on the type of purpose we pursue. Let us not forget that, like the other types of symbolic forms, language is a symbolic form. It differs from them by the fact that the meaning it communicates is conceptual in nature. Any symbolic form, and consequently any symbolic form in the fine arts, is a kind of *eidetic* language. The painter thinks in terms of pictorial images, the sculptor in terms of plastic images, the dancer in terms of dynamic images, the movie maker in terms of moving images, the novelist in terms of imaginary images, the dramatist in terms of active images, and so forth. But regardless of this difference, the content of their expression and communication is a type of meaning, something we deem important. As a kind of image, the artwork is a perceptual object. It takes a trained ear, eye, or imagination to penetrate the aesthetic dimension of the artwork and comprehend the meaning implicit in its form, and it takes a very refined ear, eye, or imagination to penetrate the aesthetic dimension of masterworks and comprehend the wealth of meaning inherent in their form.

Now, when I say that the aesthetic quality of sadness inheres in the music, I mean that it does not exist in it as a ready-made reality the way the sounds exist as physical events, and it is not identical to any of these sounds but exists in the unique way the sounds are organized as a potentiality awaiting realization in the musical experience; it exists in the dynamic interrelatedness of these sounds. The quality of sadness emerges from this dynamic interrelatedness as the sounds weave their way in the development of the musical performance. Similarly, the quality of tragedy which inheres in Jean Anouilh's *Antigone* is not given to the reader as a ready-made reality when we read the play as a story. How many students in a World Literature or Existentialism class treat this literary work as a story without noticing the gravity of the moral conflict and the dramatic depth that lie hidden in its aesthetic dimension? Again, how many readers of Dostoevsky's *The Idiot* glide over the story without noticing that Prince Myshkin is a metaphor that stands for every value and action Jesus stood for during the last three years of his life as a preacher? Do we need a direct reference to know, or see, that he is a Jesus figure? Does this type of figure not inhere in the web of scenes, characters, actions, and events that makes up the fabric of the novel? But my critic may wonder: How does this figure inhere in this web? That is, how does it communicate or reveal that Prince Myshkin is a Jesus figure without saying or declaring it explicitly?

The point I should here underscore and which I shall elaborate in Chap. 4 is that the main character in a philosophical novel (sometimes more than one character and sometimes a situation) is a metaphor that implies, signifies, or communicates a comparison with a figure that is not directly given to the reader as an analogue of the comparison; it is inferred from the kind of action that makes up the structure of the novel. What is given is the thematic conditions that are necessary for constructing the analogue. The implied character is embedded in the novel as an aesthetic object; as such, he exists as a potentiality in the novel as a significant form. The character exists as the implied world of the analogue, which is not only different from but also richer than the world of the given character. The idiot that comes to life when I read Dostoevsky's *The Idiot* as a literary work is not a simpleton or a mentally retarded human being who blundered his way into the intricate web of Russian society in the middle of the nineteenth century but a Jesus figure who pays a visit to Russian society the way Jesus paid a visit to the Jewish society about 2000 years ago. He was viewed, used, and abused the way the historical Jesus was viewed, used, and abused, that is, the way a truly loving human being is viewed, used, and abused in a society that carried the banner of love but was mired in a puddle of spiritual poverty and selfishness and was ready and willing to oppress the real Jesus once more rather than abandon their way of life. Can the reader emerge from reading this novel without asking the truly philosophical question—of whether true love is possible—and without seeing that it is hard, if not impossible, to lead a loving way of life in this world? Could Dostoevsky have disclosed this truth as vividly, as forcefully, and as luminously directly in a philosophical essay? Dostoevsky did not communicate this truth discursively; he enabled us *to see it, feel it, and to comprehend it* in the fullness of its reality.

Well, the artist can say what ordinary people cannot, or do not desire, to say explicitly or directly in ordinary life. Is this why we sometimes secretly identify ourselves with this or that character or find ourselves in this or that situation in the novel? But how can the novelist say something without "speaking" or directly expressing it? How can she veil what she wishes to say in such a way that only the reader can lift off that veil in the process of reading the novel aesthetically, or as a literary work? I believe that the ability of the artist *to say without speaking*, or to communicate what she wishes to say under a veil, is the secret of creative vision. If artistic activity is a matter of *forming* the medium in a certain way, if form is the vehicle of communicating a particular content of meaning, it should follow that the kind of meaning the artist intends to communicate must be amenable to embodiment, or expression, in a certain form. The uniqueness and structure of this meaning to a large extent determines the kind of form the artist creates. Herein lies the magic of the creative genius. Any attempt to shed rational light on this magic should take into consideration (1) the extent to which the artist understands the depth of human nature, namely, its essential needs and dynamics, because without this kind of understanding, she cannot master the needed skill in communicating the meaning it desires; and (2) the extent to which she is the master of the medium or able to subjugate it to the will of the creative vision that steers her process of artistic creation.

The relation between the artist and the medium is always dialogical. On the one hand, the kind of form the artist seeks to create depends on her knowledge of the *formation possibilities* of the medium. Discovering these possibilities is a challenge, perhaps the greatest challenge of the creative act. On the other hand, the medium offers itself as a willing and cooperative partner in this act; it offers itself as an open book the artist can read and explore. Do the words that exist in the back of the novelist's mind not advance and offer themselves as willing partners when she is trying to construct the right sentence, metaphor, image, or figure of speech? Does the right word not sometimes jump to the fore of the mind at the right time primarily because it is the right word? And can such a word resist this jump when it is lured by the seductive power of the imagination? Can the imagination seduce the word if it does not desire it?

The Aesthetic Object as a World of Meaning

If possession of significant form is what makes an artifact a work of art, if this form exists in the work as a potentiality and steps into the realm of reality in the aesthetic experience, then it should follow that its realization in the aesthetic experience transforms the artwork into an *aesthetic object*. *The Idiot* that sits next to me on the nightstand is not, as a story, a work of art because it can be read for a psychological, sociological, historical, religious, or historical purpose, not to mention the fact that it can be used as a commodity for sale or as a decorative piece on some shelf or as a means for killing time. Insofar as it is the written text in that volume, it is a potentiality for being an aesthetic object. The artwork becomes an aesthetic object in the aesthetic experience; it is the object of aesthetic appreciation and literary criticism. It reveals its true nature as art through this kind of experience. This object does not exist the way ordinary objects exist, as an experience is a subjective event. However, a careful examination of this event will readily show that it does not merely exist in the aesthetic experience but constitutes the very structure and being of the experience. *The Idiot* becomes identical with the aesthetic experience when we read it. Can we be aware of anything except the world of the novel when we give it the totality of our attention? Do we not stop being observers and become participants in its action as it unfolds in our imagination in the course of reading it? Do we not frequently identify ourselves with this or that character or find ourselves in this or that scene or situation? This is why the aesthetic object does not exist as something *external to the mind nor in it*. For example, how can we penetrate the world of *The Idiot* if we do not read the novel Dostoevsky wrote? And how can we penetrate and live in this world, albeit for a short time, if it does not become actual in our personal experience? Again, how can the art critic evaluate the novel if she does not penetrate its inner world—if she does not penetrate the web of its significant form?

Now, what do we mean when we characterize the aesthetic object as a *world of meaning*? First, what do we mean by "world"? "World" is used differently in different types of discourse. For example, we speak of the world of ideas, the mind, culture, science, or religion, and we speak of "worldview"—for example, the worldview of a certain culture, religion, ideology, philosopher, or artist. The concept of world is the concept of a whole composed of parts, in which the parts are integral to the whole. When we speak of the worldview of a certain culture, for example, we mean the unity of its beliefs, values, traditions, customs, rites, practices, and norms. But what do we mean when we characterize the aesthetic object as a world? We mean that it is a complex, diverse, and inexhaustible dimension of meaning. As I explained earlier, the realm of meaning is the realm of human values—of what we deem important in our lives. We can say that beauty, goodness, and truth and their derivatives are important; that questions of life, death, and love are important; and that any goal that aims at individual and social progress is important. The world of meaning an artwork embodies can be small, big, rich, poor, interesting, simple, or intricate. Beethoven's *Ninth Symph*ony is monumental if compared to a medieval ballad; Tolstoy's *War and Peace* is grand compared to Trollope's *The Warden*; Michaelangelo's Sistine Chapel ceiling is majestic compared to Millet's *Haystack*. But regardless of their depth, intricacy, richness, or beauty, they are worlds of meaning primarily because they are dimensions of being—spiritual being.

My critic would now ask, but is this world *real*? The tree I now see through the window of my room is real because it occupies a certain place during a stretch of time; its reality is objective. It is definable. But the aesthetic object *qua* world of meaning is not a definable object, and its reality is not objective. Accordingly, if it is real, in what sense is it real? Put differently, what is its ontological status? Let me at once say that the aesthetic object is founded in two poles: the artwork as a significant form and the subject that realizes it in her aesthetic experience. Thus, it should exist in the medium of this type of experience. But although it exists in the experience of the subject, it is not "subjective" in character but rather exists as an objectively given structure or integrity. Let me explain this claim.

The aesthetic experience is not a confused manifold of mental states—emotions, feelings, moods, ideas, images—produced in the perception of the artwork as a significant form, nor is it a kind of Damascene mosaic that exhibits a certain clarity of details and order, but a personal realization of the aesthetic possibilities inherent in the artwork as a significant form. The way these details interact with each other, their vitality or faintness, and the role they play in the unfolding of the aesthetic experience may vary from one person to another and from one aesthetic perception to another. However, regardless of how much they may vary, the kind and the general pattern of these states remain, in principle, constant because they are actuated by a basic and objectively given structure—that of the significant form—the realization of which in the aesthetic process transforms the artwork into an aesthetic object. The aesthetic experience is the realization of the aesthetic qualities inherent in the significant form. Accordingly, the structure of the experience replicates the structure of the significant form; but this form is, to a reasonable extent, an objective structure. By "structure" I mean the schema, or skeleton, that underlies the formal organization of any artwork, be it physical or mental. The stuff of this structure is the multitude of the aesthetic qualities that are expressed, or embodied, in the significant form, and they are embodied not merely in the different elements of the material medium—lines, colors, sounds, words, scenes, sounds, action, characters—but also in the way these elements are organized, or in the dynamic relations that exist between them.

However, my critic may object, if the aesthetic object exists in the aesthetic experience, do we not reduce it to a completely subjective and necessarily idiosyncratic reality? Otherwise, how can we explain the generally recognized fact that different people experience the same artwork differently? Again, if it exists in the experience of the perceiver, do we not undercut the possibility of an objective standard of evaluation and criticism? The answer to these questions is no. From the fact that the aesthetic object exists in the mind in the process of aesthetic perception, it does not necessarily follow that it exists at the idiosyncratic authority, or whim, of the mind that perceives it, just as from the fact that scientific ideas exist in the mind of the person who thinks them, it does not necessarily follow that they exist at the idiosyncratic authority, or whim, of the mind that thinks them, mainly because, as in science, the structure of the significant form, which is given as an objective reality, is the basis of the aesthetic experience. The structure of this experience is, in principle, determined by that of the significant form, which is subject to public inspection the way the scientific object is. Can we justify the possibility of art criticism as a recognized practice, and can we justify the continual appeal of the major works of art, if we do not assume the validity of this claim (see Kuczynska 2018)?

The Philosophical Novel as a Genre

If the creation and communication of meaning is what makes an activity, a text, or a work *philosophical*; if the expression and communication of meaning in a symbolic form is what makes an artifact art; and consequently, if significant form is what makes a novel a literary work of art, *what makes a literary novel a philosophical novel?* Can a literary novel be philosophical? If so, how? A number of art critics and aestheticians view novels such as Dostoevsky's *The Brothers Karamazov*, Proust's *Remembrance*, Kafka's *Metamorphosis*, Melville's *Moby Dick*, or Mann's *The Magic Mountain* as philosophical (see Goldman 2016; Descombes 1992; Porter 2004; Reyerson 2011).

The logic which underpins the possibility of the philosophical novel is, I submit, the same logic that underlies the possibility of the literary novel. But this logic, which seems clear and effective in explaining the possibility of literary novel genres such as romantic, mystery, or fantasy, does not seem to be as clear and effective in explaining the possibility of the philosophical novel. Accordingly, it is crucially important to spotlight this logic and show how it can be the basis of justifying the possibility of the philosophical novel. Let me emphasize once more that the mere presence of philosophical ideas, conversations, theories, reveries, or even characters as philosophers who express certain views on the nature of the world or human life in a novel does not necessarily make it philosophical, just as the mere presence of scientific, religious, or ideological ideas, views, or conversations in a novel does not necessarily make it scientific, religious, or ideological, just as wearing a Pakistani, Kuwaiti, or Russian dress does not necessarily make one a Pakistani, Kuwaiti, or Russian individual. A person may give brilliant philosophical lectures, write books on philosophical questions and views, and decorate her speech with philosophical gems of wisdom without necessarily *being philosophical*. We should make a distinction between wearing a philosophical garment, or having philosophical ideas or views, and being philosophical. We know whether a person is philosophical by the way she acts and interacts with her social and natural environment—that is, by the way she realizes herself as a human individual in the world, not by what she feels or says about herself, and certainly not by the way she pretends to be. She is philosophical only so far as her behavior radiates philosophicalness. How, then, does a literary novel radiate philosophicalness?

The method we should employ in answering this question is the same method we employed in answering the question of what makes an artifact art. We can argue, as I did in the previous discussion, that possession of significant form, or an aesthetic object, is what makes a literary work a *literary work of art*. But then, how does a literary work of art possess its aesthetic object? As I have already explained in some detail (see also Mitias 1987; Ingarden 1973), this object does not belong to the literary work as a perceptual aspect or as a ready-made reality in the work the artist creates but rather in the *way she forms it*. The aesthetic object inheres in this very *way-ness*. This inherence is what makes the work *expressive*; it is also what endows it with the power of communication. Aesthetic qualities such as the tragic, the demonic, the holy, the terrible, the joyful, the hopeful, the enchanting, and other types of sensory, intellectual, and psychological qualities constitute the essential structure of the aesthetic object, but this object is not exactly identical to these qualities. Unlike the work the artist produces and is given as a ready-made reality, the aesthetic object is an inexhaustible possibility of realization. Its domain is deeper, richer, and more meaningful than the domain of the given work.

Accordingly, if philosophicalness is what makes a literary novel philosophical, it should inhere in the significant form which makes it literary. In other words, it should exist in it the *way* the aesthetic object inheres in it. The point which deserves special emphasis here is that the reader of the philosophical novel does not receive its philosophical content *conceptually* or *discursively* but intuitively—by seeing it with the eye of her mind. And she can do this because she is not only a receiver in the aesthetic experience, and because she is not only a participant in it, but also she is its creator: the philosophicalness of the novel steps into the realm of reality via the imagination of the reader in the same way it is created by the imagination of the artist *qua* significant form. Just as the reader of the romantic novel experiences the power, glory, tragedy, triumph, or delight of love in the course of reading it, the reader of the philosophical novel experiences the meaning of the philosophical issue or view embodied in the significant form of the novel. We should always remember that philosophical thought originates from pre-reflective, intuitive activity, from a fundamental intuition of the nature or a dimension of meaning. This type of intuition is the birthplace of philosophical concepts, theories, or systems. As I indicated in the first two parts of this chapter, the aspect which makes this kind of activity philosophical is that it aims at the essential nature of a dimension of meaning.

Now it is time to ask more directly how the philosophical novel embodies its philosophicalness. Such a novel may, or may not, contain conceptual philosophical content, but what makes it philosophical is the extent to which philosophicalness is seen, intuited, and apprehended as a realized quality. The novel expresses and communicates this quality the same way it expresses and communicates its aesthetic-ness. It inheres in its significant form the way this form inheres in the artwork the artist created via the artistic process. Thus, just as the significant form exists in the artwork as a potentiality, philosophicalness inheres in the significant form as a potentiality. This assertion implies that it emerges in the aesthetic experience the way every aesthetic quality, including the aesthetic object, emerges, but with an added feature: philosophicalness constitutes the essential structure of this object. This constitution is what makes a literary novel philosophical. The reader does not recognize, or think it, as a conceptual content, as a description, or even as a result of logical argument in the medium of a conversation or a text but feels, sees, and apprehends it as a given concrete aesthetic event. For example, the fundamental philosophical question which permeates Tolstoy's *The Death of Ivan Ilych* is the question of the meaning of human life, and the answer he gives and which shines through the novel as an organic unity of action is that a meaningful life is an authentic life, and an authentic life is the kind of life that originates from an innocent, pure, loving heart. Similarly, the fundamental philosophical question that permeates Dostoevsky's *The Idiot* is the question of unconditional love, the kind embodied in the figure of Prince Myshkin. Dostoevsky does not say what true human love is; he *shows* us what it is, and he shows us what it is by the kind of actions Myshkin performs from the beginning of the novel to its end.

Insofar as philosophicalness inheres in the significant form of the literary novel, its ontic locus is the plot, the *way* the scenes, action, characters, and subject matter of the novel are woven into a story. Plot is the skeleton of the novel and the basis of its aesthetic dimension. We can now ask still more directly: How does a philosophical plot express its philosophicalness? Simply put, a story is an arrangement of incidents. The focus of these incidents is the action of the main characters and the social and natural scenes in which it takes place. A narrative, or a story, is about what certain human beings do and, more concretely, the types of action they perform in the course of the narrative. We know a character by what she does. Accordingly, we know the type of character she is not by what she thinks, feels, or says about herself, but by the type of action she performs in her personal, social, and professional life. For example, we know the type of character embodied by Sophocles' Oedipus by the way he acted as husband, soldier, father, citizen, warrior, and leader. We do not arrive at our knowledge of his character simply by reading the play as a story. Although we read the description of the events of the play in and through concepts, reading it aesthetically is *eidetic*, not conceptual or merely descriptive. The content of the reading is not a scientific or philosophic description of the king but a *portrayal* of his character. We read this character the way we read particular individuals in our practical lives. This character rises in the aesthetic experience as a man-in-action. Here we see this man in the fullness of his being; we see how the inner dynamics of his action—namely, thinking, feeling, and willing—are realized in his action. This is based on the assumption that an experience, *qua* experience, does not have an inner and outer dimension; it is a luminous presence.

In this type of reading, the actions are transformed into imaginative events. We intuit them directly without the aid of concepts or images; on the contrary, the character becomes a luminous image! We see Oedipus and the kind of man he is in the events which make up the thread of the narrative; we interact with him as a real person, because he exists in the imagination as a living being, and he so exists because the imaginative event in which he exists during the experience is a living, human event. This is based on the assumption, discussed earlier, that in the aesthetic experience, the sensuous in the plastic, temporal, and literary arts becomes an integral element of the aesthetic object. Thus, read as a story, *Oedipus the King* is not a tragedy—but read as a literary work art, it is. The tragic aspect of the play emerges in the aesthetic experience as a dynamic, living aspect of a living event, and it does not emerge as a mental or conceptual entity attached to the experience but as a shining presence!

It is important to emphasize at this point that the kind of plot the novelist chooses for her novel should be appropriate for the type of question, problem, or dimension of meaning she intends to communicate. The plot of a mystery novel is, to a large extent, different from that of a romantic, horror, or fantasy novel, although romance, horror, or fantasy may be elements of its plot. There are no rules for choosing a plot, mainly because the creative imagination does not recognize such rules; it creates them, and in doing so it generates a style, a trend, or a school in artistic expression. The history of literature contains an amazing mosaic of tragic and other types of plots. What matters in the case of the philosophical novel is the kind of narrative that enables the artist to communicate a philosophical insight, attitude, vision, or understanding of a basic dimension of meaning.

But my critic might now step in with an objection. In a romantic, horror, or mystery novel, for example, the focus is on action primarily because these genres are founded in action or in relationships, but philosophy is essentially an activity of the mind. How can a plot be philosophical? It can be! The capacity of a plot to be philosophical is, in principle, similar to its capacity to be romantic, horrifying, or mysterious. Just as the tragic quality in *Oedipus the King* is embedded in its characters and the kind of actions that make up the structure of the play, the philosophical aspect of a novel is embodied in the action of a character or characters. The philosophical character or situation radiates philosophicalness the way Oedipus the king radiates tragic-ness or the way Prince Myshkin radiates love. We read the quality in the character eidetically, even in a philosophical text or conversation, if the novel happens to contain such texts or conversations. I intuit and comprehend philosophicalness in the process of creating the events and characters of the novel in my imagination; I *see* it in them the way I see the beauty of a character or a landscape. This kind of experience is not mediated by any concepts, arguments, analogies, or images. In it I become one with the experience. Although for a short time, I take a break from the course of ordinary life and live the tragic aspect of Oedipus' life primarily because I am one with him in the medium of the aesthetic experience.

It is extremely difficult for the serious reader of a literary novel to remain unmoved or unchanged after she reads works such as Dostoevsky's *The Brothers Karamazov* or Melville's *Moby Dick*. If the novelist aims first and foremost at the truth of a dimension of meaning of the world and human life, if this aim points to a human being committed to a life of growth and development, if reading the work necessarily involves creating the meaning and, in creating it, the reader lives it, how can she remain silent after reading such novels? Is there not a profound desire in human nature to seek the meaning of human life and live according to it? Is there not an impulse in us to be what we should be—that is, to be authentic? Again, do we not aim at the truth in the different spheres of our lives: family, friendship, marriage, business, work? Do we not frown upon liars and respect honest human beings? Do we not stop reading a book if we suddenly discover that it does not aim at the truth?

Now, if novels are literary inasmuch as they embody aesthetic qualities; if they are romantic, mystery, horror, or fantasy novels inasmuch as their dominant aesthetic quality is romantic, mystery, horror, or fantasy in nature, and as such literary genres; if, like the philosophical work, the artwork is an expression and communication of the truth of a dimension of meaning of the world and human life; and finally, if philosophicalness can be embodied as a dominant aesthetic quality in a novel, as the preceding discussion in its entirety has shown, it should follow that novels that embody philosophicalness as a dominant aesthetic quality such as Tolstoy's *The Death of Ivan Ilych*, Melville's *Moby Dick*, Proust's *Remembrance*, Maugham's *Of Human Bondage*, Kafka's *Metamorphosis*, or Mann's *The Magic Mountain* can be viewed as a genre.

References and Suggested Bibliography

Bell, Clive (1958). *Art*. New York: Capricorn Books.
Descombes, Vincent (1992). *Proust: Philosophy of the Novel*. Translated by Catherine C. Beardsley. Stanford: Stanford University Press.
Dufrenne, Mikel (1973). *Phenomenology of Aesthetic Experience*. Evanston: Northwestern University Press.
Goldman, Alan H. (2016). *Philosophy and the Novel*. Oxford: Oxford University Press.
Ingarden, Roman (1973). *The Literary Work of Art, Evanston*. Iniana: Northewestern University Press.

Kuczynska, Alicja (2018). *Art as a Philosophy*, in *Dialogue and Universalism*, issue 28; (1988); "Qualities of Things and Aesthetic qualities," in Mitias (1988), *Aesthetic Quality and Aesthetic Experience*.

Mitias, Michael. (1987). *What Makes an Experience Aesthetic?* Rodopi; *The Possibility of Aesthetic Experience*. Amsterdam: *Kluwer, 1987*; *Aesthetic Quality and Aesthetic Experience*. Amsterdam: Rodopi, 1988; *The Philosopher and the Devil*, London: Olympia, 2018.

Porter, Burton (2004). *Philosophy Through Fiction and Film*. Upper Sadler River: Pearson Prentice-Hall.

Reyerson, James (2011). "The Philosophical Novel." New York: *New York Times Sunday Book Review*.

CHAPTER 4

How the Philosophical Novel Communicates Knowledge

I have so far argued that, as a literary work of art, the philosophical novel should be treated as a genre; accordingly, it should stand on par with genres such as romantic, adventure, mystery, or picaresque novels, primarily because it has the basic elements and features that make it a *type*. This proposition is supported by five basic assumptions. *First*, aesthetic quality is the basis of *artistic distinction*: an artifact is art inasmuch as it possesses aesthetic qualities. Thus, an analysis of an "artwork," "aesthetic experience," "artistic creation," or "artistic criticism and evaluation" would entail an adequate understanding of the essential nature, mode of existence, the relation of aesthetic quality to other types of qualities, and the role of art in human life and civilization. *Second*, aesthetic quality is the basis of *literary distinction*: a poem, a novel, an epic, a short story, or a play is a literary work of art inasmuch as it possesses aesthetic qualities. The absence of these qualities from these types of works precludes them from inclusion in the category of literature: "the aesthetic" defines "the literary." Accordingly, an analysis of the literary dimension of a literary work of art is, in effect, an analysis of its aesthetic dimension. *Third*, aesthetic qualities are not given to sensuous or imaginary perceptions as ready-made realities the way rocks, trees, colors, representations, sentences, or motions are given; they inhere in the artwork as potentialities awaiting realization in the aesthetic experience. Their unity in the artwork is what aestheticians usually call "significant form." This form emerges as an *aesthetic object* in the process of perceiving the work aesthetically. It is the primary aim of the

© The Author(s), under exclusive license to Springer Nature Switzerland AG 2022
M. H. Mitias, *The Philosophical Novel as a Literary Genre*,
https://doi.org/10.1007/978-3-030-97385-8_4

artist in the activity of artistic creation and of the perceiver in the activity of perceiving the artwork aesthetically. *Fourth*, the theme of an artwork is the principle of *genre distinction*. The theme of a literary novel determines its inclusion or exclusion from a certain genre. It is fantasy, romantic, or adventure if its theme is fantasy, romance, or adventure. However, the theme does not exist in the novel as a conceptually articulated or thought narrative but as an aesthetically expressed, felt, or intuited content. It exists in the novel as a significant form and in the aesthetic experience as an aesthetic object. *Fifth*, the philosophical novel exists as a genre on par with the generally recognized genres because it is possible for the theme of the literary novel to be philosophical. This assertion is based on the generally recognized principle that the theme of an artwork is the basis of genre distinction or identity and of creating a new genre the way science fiction was first recognized as a genre a few decades ago. The dominant theme of a literary novel is not only a viable possibility; it is, as I shall discuss, the dominant theme of some of the most important novels in the realm of literature.

The mere statement of the fifth proposition would, I think, raise the skeptical eyebrows of many aestheticians, literary theorists, and critics. How can a literary novel be philosophical? If it can, how can it communicate philosophical knowledge? The thesis of this chapter is that it can, like a philosophical work, communicate philosophical knowledge. My approach to responding to these questions will consist of two parts: first, I shall elucidate the fifth proposition, and, second, I shall articulate the objections of my critic. The remainder of this chapter will be devoted to a detailed analysis of and responses to these objections.

First, an elucidation of the fifth proposition. If a literary novel can be philosophical, a critic would ask, then its theme cannot be presumed as a ready-made reality, that is, as an articulated conceptual or propositional structure, one the reader thinks or conceives but as a potentiality awaiting realization in the event of reading the novel aesthetically. However, concepts are intellectual constructs; as such, they are given to us as ready-made realities. We do not construct a philosophical text; we try to understand it. Its meaning is implicit in it. We do not create its meaning; we try to explore and comprehend it. The philosophical texts we ordinarily read are composed of a propositional structure or one that can be reduced to propositions. We may misunderstand or misinterpret it, but the mistake can be corrected. A critic, a commentator, or the author can correct our mistake or shed light on it. This is possible only because the author has determined the parameters of its meaning according to established linguistic and philosophical rules and conventions. Much, if not most, of the writing done in the world of philosophy is a series of comments, criticisms, evaluations, clarifications, or elucidations of the ideas of the major philosophers. How can this type of activity take place if the meaning of these ideas is not given as a ready-made reality?

However, the philosophical content of a philosophical novel is not given as a conceptual or propositional content but as the unity of the aesthetic qualities, viz., as a significant form, which emerges as an aesthetic object in the aesthetic experience. This object is not, as I shall explain in detail in the next part of this chapter, a conceptual structure; on the contrary, it is a world of meaning, primarily because the aesthetic qualities that inhere in the artwork *qua* potentialities come to life in the aesthetic experience as pure meaning. This meaning cannot be reduced to a concept, feeling, or any type of intuition completely. It is a drop of experience, as Whitehead has emphasized, or spiritual moment, as Hegel has argued. We may articulate the world of the novel conceptually, as critics, commentators, and aestheticians do, but our conceptualization will never capture it in the fullness of its being; it defies complete or final conceptualization because the values inherent in the world of the novel are an inexhaustible source of realization. However, on the other hand, if we can conceptually articulate its meaning in the fullness of its being, we necessarily reduce the novel to a philosophical or perhaps to a scientific text. The novel would, in other words, cease to be a literary work of art. Do we not, in a moment of imaginary calm, stand in awe, reflective silence, silent confusion, vibrancy, or a mystical mood after we finish reading serious novels such as Melville's *Moby Dick,* Gogol's *Dead Souls,* Dostoevsky's *The Brothers Karamazov,* or Proust's *Remembrance?* Do we not feel enlightened or have a Eureka experience when we read such novels? For example, do we not grasp the question of the meaning of human life when we read Tolstoy's *The Death of Ivan Ilyich?* Do we not witness a panorama of fraudulence in all its cunning, whims, caprice, and sarcasm when we read Gogol's *Dead Souls?* In short, do we not learn more about the question of the meaning of human life from reading such novels than from reading philosophers' books or hearing their lectures?

The following remarks are now in order. Unlike reading philosophy books, which takes place at the level of the intellect, that is, at the level of abstract thought, reading a philosophical novel is an invitation to be an actor in the world of the novel, to be an actor in it. The reader not only acts as a spectator of this world but also as an actor in it and, more importantly, as its creator, for its theme is not given as a ready-made reality but as a potentiality to be realized by the reader in the event of reading it. This activity is a type of creation *par excellence*. It begins when we read the first sentence and ends when we read the last sentence. This is based on the firm assumption that different people read the same novel differently and on the fact that the novel does not exist outside the event of reading it. Moreover, the *Death of Ivan Ilych* that sits at the right side of my desk is not exactly the novel Tolstoy created. It is speechless and lifeless. What sits on my desk is a large mass of marks organized according to literary and philosophical rules and conventions. They carry on their wings the potentiality of a world; but as a potentiality, they are a limitless source of realization. Even the novelist who wrote the novel cannot set limits to the range of this realization. As Matisse once said, the artist stands in relation to their work the way critics do. How they create the potentiality of a world, one that is a limitless source of expansion, is one of the wondrous mysteries of the creative act. If this is the case, and I think it is, it would be reasonable to say that an aesthetic reading of the philosophical novel is essentially an activity of creating a human world.

In this kind of activity, the reader is not, and cannot be, only an actor but also a spectator: for example, how can a novelist create a character if she does not know what it means to be that very character and if they do not model it according to the vision that steered their creative process? And, how can they do this without intuiting and appreciating the aesthetic dimension she is creating? Are this intuition and appreciation not integral parts of creating the novel? After all, should the novel not originate from a genuine literary and human mind and heart?

I am not unaware of the paradoxical nature of the claim that the aesthetic reader of the philosophical novel is at once an observer and a creator in the process of reading the novel, for it would seem that the activity of creating logically precludes the activity of observing and appreciating: How can one appreciate when one is immersed in the activity of creation? My critic might remind me that, whether it is in the capacity of artist or aesthetic reader, the creator may enjoy the activity of creation when it is taking place, but this type of enjoyment is different from the enjoyment of the novel *qua* aesthetic object. I own this difference, but I should immediately remind the critic that the laws of formal logic do not apply to the laws of artistic creation, perception, and appreciation, which are dialectical, not syllogistic, in nature. How can a novelist write the last sentence of a novel without a smile or a nod of approval if they are not certain that the novel they have just written is meaningful or pleasing? The paradox involved in creating and experiencing a literary novel aesthetically is, I concede, an existential paradox, in the sense that it is given as such and experienced and appreciated as such.

Second, articulation of the critic's objections. (A) The first focus of my critic would be the subject of the philosophical novel and that of the philosophical work. I may be told that the subject of reflection in philosophy is reality; the subject of a philosophical novel is an imaginary world. The philosopher aims to interpret the real world; the philosophical novelist aims to create one. The real world is given; the world of the novelist is possible. The real world exists as a part of the cosmic process; the world of the novelist exists in the mind of the novelist. The question we should here ask is, "How can an imaginary work make a cognitive contribution about the real world? How can two radically different worlds that are expressed in different symbolic languages communicate with each other?" (B) The second focus of my critic would be the aim of the philosopher and that of the philosophical novelist. First, what is the aim of the philosopher? The empirical scientist aims to know the facts that make up the scheme of nature; the philosopher aims to know the *meaning* of these facts: What is the purpose of existence in general and the purpose of human existence in particular? How should we live? Does a personal God exist? What is mind or human nature? Again, what is the nature of beauty, love, justice, courage, or happiness? What is the best form of social organization? However, if the aim of the philosopher is to examine and shed light on the meaning of the *real* world, and if the aim of the philosophical novelist, *qua* novelist, is to create a *fictional* world, how can they shed a light of understanding on the meaning of the world? In other words, can a philosophical novelist perform the function of a philosopher and at the same time remain a philosophical novelist? We should not forget that philosophical knowledge is presented through the medium of concepts or propositions, while literary knowledge is presented through the medium of intuition or feeling. The first is achieved by means of logical and empirical argument, while the second is presented as a point of view. The first is subject to a rigorous process of verification, while the second is not. The first can be true or false, while the second cannot. (C) The third focus of my critic is the method by which the philosopher arrives at their knowledge in contrast to the philosophical novelist. Both start from what we may call *pre-reflective or pre-symbolic intuition* of the meaning implicit in human and natural objects. This intuition is founded in (a) the comprehensive contemplation of the mystery, complexity, infinity, and exuberant design of the human and natural orders and (b) the most recent and most adequate scientific knowledge of these orders. Although affective and indeterminate in its structure, it is cognitive in character. If it were not cognitive, it would not be the basis, or source, of any type of symbolic knowledge or expression, and yet it is the source of any hunch, hypothesis, or speculation about any aspect of the human and natural worlds. The knowledge that dwells in the womb of this pre-reflective level of intuition is not scientific, artistic, philosophical, or religious, and it does not exist in any mode of symbolic expression; yet, it is a potentiality for expression by these and other modes of human expression. The method the philosopher uses to communicate their understanding of an aspect of the meaning of human or natural reality is, as we saw a moment ago, conceptual and propositional; it is essentially different from the method the philosophical novelist uses to express their understanding of the same meaning, assuming that they understand it similarly. This is based on the assumption that the meaning inherent in the intuition of a certain aspect of reality is a potentiality for realization through different modes of symbolic expression. However, my critic would wonder: Is it really possible for the same content of meaning to be communicated in two different modes of expression? For example, what is the use of writing a philosophical novel whose theme is the ugliness of death if the theme can be communicated, or expressed, by the philosopher? But then, can the philosophical novelist express the same meaning the philosopher seeks to express conceptually? Or, can the philosopher express the same meaning the philosophical novelist can express? Can they intuit the ugliness of death, or its truth, in the same way? Do we learn more, less, or something different, if we read a philosophical novel after we read a philosophical text on the same subject?

The preceding three skeptical reactions have been advanced against the thesis that the genre of the philosophical novel is possible and that the kind of knowledge it communicates is not essentially different from the kind the philosopher seeks and communicates. This thesis is based on the assumption that if the dominant theme of a literary novel is or can be philosophical, in the sense that it seeks to capture the same truth the philosopher seeks to capture, then it is not only a genre but also expresses the same kind of knowledge the philosopher seeks to communicate. However, arguing that a literary novel can be philosophical is not enough. We should also answer the following question: How can a philosophical novel communicate philosophical knowledge or understanding? How can a *depictive* work communicate the kind of truth or meaning inherent in a conceptual or propositional construct? Again, how can a literary novel be philosophical without losing its literary identity? Many aestheticians, art critics, and literary theorists seek to grasp the meaning of aspects of human and natural reality as lucidly as possible, each in its own way, but the question that merits urgent attention, my critic insists, is whether, and how, the philosophical novel can communicate the kind of knowledge the philosopher endeavors to communicate?

My answer to this question is yes: the kind of knowledge or understanding the philosophical novel communicates is not different from the kind of knowledge or understanding the philosophical work communicates. I shall, in the remainder of this chapter, elucidate and defend this proposition. The defense will be composed of three parts. *First*, I shall advance an analysis of the principle of literary distinction. Here, I shall argue that the possession of aesthetic qualities is what makes an artifact a work of art. Accordingly, a novel that possesses aesthetic qualities is a literary work of art. Its theme is the principle of genre distinction: a novel is philosophical if its dominant theme is philosophical in nature. *Second*, the theme of the philosophical novel emerges as an aesthetic object in the course of the aesthetic experience. The building blocks of this object is the unity of the realized aesthetic qualities that make up the structure of the artwork as a significant form. This object comes to life in the aesthetic experience. Its realization is the locus in and through which the philosophical novel communicates the knowledge inherent in it. I here assume that an understanding of how a literary novel embodies its philosophical theme and how the theme is realized in the aesthetic experience is a necessary condition for an adequate explanation of the conditions under which a literary novel can communicate philosophical understanding. The proposition I shall propose and support is that the point of a philosophical work is to disclose the truth of the meaning of an aspect of reality. Similarly, the point of a philosophical novelist's reliance on figures of speech or any kind of depiction is to disclose the truth of the meaning of an aspect of reality. Depiction and conception are means to one end: the end is understanding an aspect of reality. *Third*, I shall provide a defense of my thesis, that philosophical novels communicate knowledge, using an analysis of Dostoevsky's *The Grand Inquisitor* scene in *The Brothers Karamazov*.

Artwork and Aesthetic Object

Unlike the object of science or ordinary experience, the artwork *qua art* is not given directly to our sensuous or imaginary perception as a ready-made object. The object I see on the other side of my desk is a chair. It is a chair and nothing else. Its "chair-ness" shines through its very shape and presence to my senses. However, what I directly see when I look at the brown statue of a beautiful woman that stands grandly on a pedestal in the corner of my room is not only a physical object but also a work of art. I see two contemplative eyes gaping into the distance, gracefully combed hair, two robust breasts radiating life, a piglet cozily sitting within her right arm over an elegant skirt flying on the back of a gentle breeze. This goddess is a symbol of fertility. However, I do not see a tag at the base of the pedestal saying "Goddess of Fertility" or a symbol declaring it a work of art. The goddess I see transcends the physical statue that sits on the pedestal. The deeper I move into the artistic dimension of this statue, the more I find myself in the presence of a goddess! This kind of perception applies to the multitudes of the works that fill museums, art centers, theaters, literary books, or dance halls throughout the world. Ordinary perception does not deliver the artistic dimension of the artwork. This dimension exists as a potentiality in the work the artist creates. As I shall explain in detail later, penetrating this dimension requires another kind of perception. First, how does the artistic dimension exist in the sensuously or imaginatively given artwork? Second, how does it become actual in our perception of the given work? What kind of reality is the object, or content, that results from this perception?

Let me, *first*, reiterate that the basis of artistic distinction is the possession of aesthetic qualities; their presence on an artwork is what makes it *art*. These qualities are not directly given to ordinary perception as ready-made realities. They inhere as potentialities in the form of the work the artist has created; they emerge in the aesthetic experience as a web of meaning. Their unity in the artwork is referred to by many aestheticians as a "significant form," a form that has the capacity to communicate or express aesthetic values. They do not inhere in the form simpliciter, or *simplicitas*, in the sense that we perceive them directly but *in the way the form is organized by the artist*. The possibilities of creating significant forms in the different artistic media are infinite. For example, words, lines and colors, marble, or motions can be formed in different ways. Nevertheless, the significant form is the kind of form that carries in its *way-ness* the possibilities of different aesthetic qualities; however, these qualities do not, in general, exist as sensuous features. Accordingly, we do not encounter an abstract significant form in the real world but particular, concrete significant forms embodied in particular artworks, for example, Conrad's *The Heart of Darkness* or the *Cathedral of St. Paul* in London.

The significant form is, moreover, *the locus* of the theme of an artwork. This theme is not given as a ready-made reality primarily because the significant form in which it inheres exists as a potentiality in the artwork. We do not see enigma, wonder, thoughtfulness, anxiety, or irony when we cast an ordinary look at Davinci's *Mona Lisa*. What we see is a woman looking in a certain way. The aesthetic qualities that make it art are the basis of its theme; we have to penetrate into the unique form of the representation to discover the theme potential in it. This discovery is, as I shall explain, an activity of creation. The significant form is the language by which the artist speaks and by which they communicate their message, viz., the theme. However, this language is *eidetic* in character. The painter speaks pictorially, the novelist speaks linguistically, the musician speaks musically, and the dancer speaks dynamically. Just as words or sentences are the means by which the philosopher, the scientist, and the theologian speak, the significant form is the means by which the artist speaks.

Let me, *second*, submit that an artwork comes to life as art, that is, it becomes real in contrast to its earlier, potential existence in a given artwork through aesthetic experience. This kind of experience is its ontic locus; it is the domain of its existence. However, this domain is subjective and temporary because reality, in general, and human experience, in particular, are in constant flux; although it is temporary, it nevertheless endures because it inheres as a potentiality in the significant form that endures in the artwork; although its mode of existence is subjective, it is neither idiosyncratic nor personal; moreover, although its ontic locus is subjective, it is also objective because it is founded in the significant form that inheres in the artwork as an objective structure. The aesthetic perceiver enables it to step into the realm of reality because they deem it important and because they cherish the satisfaction they derive from it. However, this kind of experience and satisfaction is not exclusive to this or that aesthetic perceiver, regardless of their professional, educational, or intellectual endowments but is available to anyone who is interested in the kind of value experience the artwork communicates.

Now, how does the artistic dimension of the artwork undergo a change of its ontic status, from being a potentiality to being an actuality? What kind of ontic identity does this dimension acquire in this change? This is a critically important question because the mode of existence of potentiality is different from that of reality. Besides, potentiality is an indeterminate existence, while reality is always a concrete, definable existence. How do we know that the concretization of an indeterminate reality is reflected correctly in any one of its concretizations? Alas! How can we distinguish an ordinary object from a work of art? I raise this question because the work the artist produces is, in fact, an ordinary object: What kind of perception sees, gleans, or discerns that a significant form lurks within its given form?

Broadly, we learn how to distinguish artworks from ordinary artifacts by what we may call "aesthetic sense"; it is a kind of aesthetic eye or ear that enables us to see, feel, or recognize certain types of aesthetic qualities the way ordinary eyes and ears enable us to see or recognize sensuous qualities. The artwork is not, as I insisted earlier, an ordinary object; it is an immediately felt or intuited object. We know or discover aesthetic qualities by perceiving not by thinking or applying rules of perception. It would be difficult for a person to perceive an aesthetic quality in a work of art if they do not possess an aesthetic sense. Usually, such perception is sparked by a special aspect—quality, radiance, or emphasis—that lures the perceiver to explore its significance or possible aesthetic promise and gradually probe the significant form that lies hidden behind or within the given form. I should here underscore the fact that this aspect, which points to the artistic dimension of the artwork, is not blank; it is, to some extent, an aesthetic depth. It functions as an introduction to the aesthetic perception of the artwork.

The aesthetic experience begins when aesthetic perception begins. In this kind of perception, the artistic dimension of the artwork is transformed into an aesthetic dimension because what existed in the artwork as artistic qualities now exists in the experience as perceived qualities. What was general, abstract, and potential is now particular, concrete, and real. The structure of the significant form constitutes the essential structure of the aesthetic experience. The aesthetic domain of the experience reflects the artistic domain of the artwork. I should hasten to add at this point of my discussion that the aesthetic perception of the physical dimension of the artwork—marble, lines and colors, motion, or sound—becomes a part of the experience because the significant form inheres in it, in the kind of qualities that make up the being of the artwork. In the aesthetic experience that which is physical is spiritualized; it undergoes a change of identity. It is, as I pointed out earlier, neither physical nor psychological in character but a pure experience. For example, are we aware of our bodies, physical environment, pains, pleasures, or the concerns of our practical life when we are in the heat of writing a letter to a dear friend or in the heat of a creative act, loving act, reflective act, or an exciting conversation? No. The category of experience is generically different from the category of the physical or the psychological as such.

It is appropriate to characterize the physical dimension of the artwork as the *vehicle* of aesthetic experience for three reasons: first, the significant form inheres in it; second, it is an essential element of the significant form; and third, it provides the fundamental structure according to which the experience is organized. It, in effect, says to the aesthetic perceiver, "In your experience of the artwork, you cannot stray from the significant form inherent in me." It contains the structure that steers the unfolding of the aesthetic experience. Another reason why we cannot stray from the parameters of the significant form is that it is the locus of the theme of the artwork. The unity of the theme is implied by the unity of the significant form.

First, the unfolding of the aesthetic experience does not take place randomly, idiosyncratically, or at the whim of the perceiver but systematically according to the logic implicit in the significant form. It is the same logic that is immanent in the vision of the creative process, that is, the process in which the artist transforms their medium into a work of art. The perception of a quality as being aesthetic signifies the emergence of an element in the course of the aesthetic experience. Indeed, the logic of the creative vision, which is the driving force of the creative process, is also the driving force of the aesthetic experience. *Second,* the unfolding of the aesthetic experience is both a developmental and an accumulative process. It begins with the perception of the qualities that make up the fabric of the artwork, but this beginning should not be taken lightly because the significant form is immanent in their unity. As I have just explained, something about these qualities opens a door that leads to its wider domain. The more one's perception of the work expands, the deeper they penetrate the aesthetic dimension both qualitatively and quantitatively. The aesthetic experience begins to unfold when aesthetic perception starts to generate this depth. This beginning marks the emergence of the aesthetic attitude in which the perceiver takes a break from ordinary perception and focuses the totality of their attention on the aesthetic dimension of the artwork. They bracket the ordinary world and move into the depth of this dimension. The deeper they move into the aesthetic dimension of the work, the farther they move from the ordinary world. This type of perception is characterized as "aesthetic" in contrast to the kind characterized as "ordinary" primarily because it is the perception of aesthetic qualities and because these values exist exclusively in the domain of the aesthetic experience. It is a perception of emergent qualities, of qualities that come into being by a creative act of the perceiver.

Regardless of whether it is musical, sculptural, literary, or pictorial, the artistic dimension of the artwork exists as the unity of its artistic qualities; these qualities are realized as a spiritual reality in the aesthetic experience. The domain of this reality is the domain of the *aesthetic object*. We can justifiably refer to it as a "world" because it is the realization of the themes inherent in the artwork. As we shall presently see, this is a diverse multiplicity of the elements that emerge in the aesthetic experience. This world can be small or large, simple or complex, impenetrable, or easy to penetrate. Moreover, it can be comic, tragic, romantic, mysterious, fantastical, monstrous, joyful, or exhilarating. In short, it can assume any of the values that are important to human beings. I do not exaggerate if I say that the work exists for the sake of these values or aspects of human life. The glory of the artistic qualities is that they disclose the significance, vibrancy, and the role human values play in human progress and satisfaction. We go to museums, theaters, musical, and dance halls, and we read literary works primarily because we deem them valuable, because they reveal through these values the fullness of their being and truth. In the aesthetic experience, we see, feel, know, and appreciate what it means for a person, situation, ideal, project, or action to be moral, ugly, horrible, loving, or disgusting! These values exist as potentialities in the fabric of the artwork as art. Their pursuit is not merely a source of understanding the meaning of human life but also of what makes it tick—exciting, interesting, challenging, and sometimes thrilling. How can a life be worth living without knowing what it means to love, hate, and confront the horrible, the terrible, the disgusting, or the courageous?

The artwork is composed of three distinct strata: the vehicle, artistic qualities, and human values (see Mitias 1987). The vehicle refers to the physical work the artist produces in the process of artistic creation. The aesthetic qualities are the qualities that make up the artistic dimension of the work, and the human values refer to the dimension of meaning inherent in the artistic dimension. The aesthetic dimension of the artwork exists as a potentiality in the fabric of the artistic dimension. They inhere in the artwork as a significant form. The aesthetic experience is the medium in which the theme of the work emerges as a real object. Let me illustrate this pivotal point by an example: DaVinci's *Mona Lisa*. The first thing I see when I approach this painting with the intention of perceiving it aesthetically is the representation of a woman seated in front of a spacious, aerial landscape looking into an indefinite space. Her right hand is placed over her left hand. I can also see the mosaic of details that make up the representation. Can my eyes see anything else? No. They can describe the richness of the details, but they cannot attribute any other feature to it primarily because the ordinary eye, or any other sense, can perceive but cannot interpret, judge, or valuate. However, something about this representation lures my eyes from the ordinary to the aesthetic mode of perception—the eyes, the lips, the posture of the hands, or an element of the given representation, for example, its special depth or the way the woman sits in the middle of that painting! For instance, instead of merely seeing a look, I may see an intriguing, mystifying look, one that is focused everywhere but nowhere: at me, the person who stands before her, and at every point of the space that envelopes me—or, could it be that she is looking at the infinite through the space that envelopes me or perhaps the space that envelopes her? Could it be that her look is aiming at the depth of this infinity? Could it be those eyes are seeking the creator of this infinity, if there is one? But how can this kind of look, this very look, lure me away from the mode of ordinary perception, away from the ordinary world, into a different world and different mode of perception? The eyes are one element of the representation; it is a part of the head, and the head is a part of the scene that constitutes the artistic structure of the representation as a whole. It is difficult for me to perceive any one element in isolation. Whether directly or indirectly, I see the eyes in terms of the whole of which they are a part. However, this whole is an organic unity. The sensuous and artistic identity of these parts is determined by its organic interrelatedness.

Accordingly, the intriguing, mystifying quality of Mona Lisa's look, which exists as a potentiality in the unique, significant organization of the representation, cannot be perceived apart from the artistic identity of the other parts of the painting. How can that smile speak to me if it is not an integral part of that human—of a living face, a face that speaks? Moreover, how can that face speak if every element and every configuration of the face do not speak? However, my aesthetic eyes that lift the veil off the hidden look that exists in the given painting as a passive formation of lines and colors also lifts, albeit gradually, the veil off an intriguing smile that radiates enigma. This smile is as mystifying and as intriguing as the look, as if that look is in dialogue with the smile, as if what the eyes are *seeing* is what the lips are *saying*! Why would the lips of a human being who travels into the infinite depth, into the *horizon of all horizons*, smile that mystifying, enigmatic smile? How can Mona Lisa express it if she does not have a vision and an understanding of the terrifying abysmal darkness of the infinite? Does the enigma and mystery that ooze out of that smile not originate from that vision? Alas, can we stand at that horizon without *smiling that* smile? However, Mona's smile is neither cheerful nor happy, it is neither angry nor sad, and it is neither philosophical nor poetic. It is enigmatic! Is it enigmatic because it radiates *uncertainty*, not about this or that situation or expectation, but the universal uncertainty of the human condition? Why not? How would you feel if, while standing at that horizon, you cast a reflective look at the cosmic stage where human beings and everything that exists comes onto it through one door and sooner than the blink of an eye leave it through another door—into that abysmal darkness? Yes, dear reader, how would you feel if you stand at that horizon and cast a reflective look at the drama enacted on that stage and then, dialectically, at that terrifying darkness? How would you feel if this darkness that enfolds the universe is all there is or can be? Could it be that the conversation between the look and the smile discloses one of the most dramatic secrets of human life and destiny? Could it be that in this smile and this look DaVinci has pictorially invited the aesthetic perceiver to take a break from the ordinary concerns of their life and examine its meaning or destiny?

It is not my intention to advance a critical and evaluative analysis of the *Mona Lisa* but only to spotlight the dynamics of aesthetic perception and the conditions under which the aesthetic experience unfolds in this kind of perception. Toward this end, four remarks deserve special emphasis: first, the emergence of the aesthetic object is the culmination of the aesthetic experience, second, the fabric of this object consists of the realized aesthetic qualities that make up the fabric of the significant form, third, the aesthetic object emerges out of the values that inhere in these realized qualities, and, fourth, the aesthetic object is a world of meaning because it is the unity of the values that emerge from the realization of these qualities.

How Does the Philosophical Novel Communicate Knowledge?

One of the recalcitrant questions that occupied the attention of the philosophers of literature during the past two decades is whether the literary work in general can communicate knowledge, and if it can, what kind of knowledge can it communicate? While some have defended the proposition that a literary work, in general, and a literary novel, in particular, can communicate significant knowledge, others have argued against it. However, the debate between the proponents and opponents of this proposition will be more critical, more heated, and more contentious, and perhaps more divisive if a theoretician such as the writer of this book submits a new version of this proposition, namely, the *philosophical novel is a literary genre,* and this type of literary novel can communicate philosophical knowledge. Broadly speaking, the discussion of this question has been critical, constructive, and insightful. It is still underway, and I doubt that it will abate in the near future mainly because art in general, and especially the literary novel, has been, next to philosophy and science, one of the central means of human *expression and communication* ever since the dawn of human civilization in the East and the West. What is the purpose of creating poems, plays, novels, aesthetic prose, and short stories? Entertainment, regardless of how lofty or mundane they might be? Killing time? A means of education in school? Flight from the oppressive noise and pressures of ordinary life? In short, is it a means to a practical end? I am inclined to think that the literary work can perform these and other practical functions but that their primary aim or function is that they are fundamental means of human expression and communication, and they are such means because they are embodiments of intrinsic values—intellectual, moral, religious, political, metaphysical, and cultural values. A value is intrinsic, that is, essentially important, inasmuch as it is an existential response to an essential or basic demand or aspiration of human nature, for example, love, knowledge, beauty, justice, freedom, or courage. We become the human beings we should be when we realize these and similar values in our individual lives.

In themselves, values exist as schemas, ideals, or plans of action. This mode of existence is general, abstract, and conceptual. This is why I characterized their existence in the first part of this chapter as being potential. They exist concretely in the sphere of reality as embodiments, and the locus of these embodiments are the qualities of actions, situations, and objects. They come to life when people experience these qualities. For example, when I watch a mother caring for her sick child, I can say that her action is one of love. Here, I imply that the action is a realization of the value of love in her action. As schemas, values do not actually exist in the world. Natural objects are value-free; they are brute facts. They are neither good nor bad, neither beautiful nor ugly, and neither useful nor useless. Consider values such as justice, honesty, or beauty. We do not see these values stacked on a shelf in a department store nor taking a walk in the park. What we see is just actions or laws, beautiful objects or individuals, or honest human beings or companies. This general claim is corroborated by the assumption that, as plans of action, values are possibilities of limitless types, forms, ways of realization primarily because they are general and because their realization takes place in concrete, particular situations. A realization is a concretization of a general or universal; it is the translation of a general or universal judgment into a singular one. It depends on the nature of one's needs, intelligence, and the cultural and social conditions under which the realization takes place. However, what matters in this discussion is that an intrinsic value represents a response to a fundamental human need and that its intrinsicality is derived from the generally accepted belief that humanity exists as an end in itself: every aim, desire, need, or pursuit is intrinsically valuable inasmuch as it promotes human wellbeing.

The domain of values is the domain *of meaning*, of what matters to people as human beings. Their realization in experience is what makes the life of a person worth living. The point I should here emphasize is that the reason for being of the literary novelist and the aesthetic reader is the expression and appreciation of human values. A corollary to this assertion is that if the literary novel, in general, and the philosophical novel, in particular, communicate knowledge, the stratum of aesthetic values should be the basis and means of this kind of communication. Accordingly, *the kind of knowledge the literary novel communicates is determined by its theme*, which may be romantic, religious, adventure, fantasy, or political in nature. Here, my critic, who has been following the line of my thinking to this very point, would interject, "I understand what you mean when you say that a literary novel can be romantic because its romantic theme can be depicted in the medium of action, the way, for example, it is depicted in *Wuthering Heights*, Tolstoy's *Anna Karenina*, or Hardy's *Far from the Madding Crowd*. However, how can a novelist depict philosophicalness? As you pointed out more than once, philosophy is an activity of thinking. This activity is subjective; it is hidden within the walls of the mind. How can the novelist enter this kind of mind and depict the philosophical activity it undergoes? They can enter their own mind, but the human mind as such, or the philosophical mind? Maybe if they are a philosopher, but what if they are not? However, even if they are a philosopher, can they depict their train of thought? More concretely, how can an argument or a demonstration, which are the essential ingredients of philosophical activity, be depicted or expressed figuratively? Suppose a train of thought concludes with a truth or a proposition, how can they depict this truth or proposition? In a philosophical work, I follow the line of reasoning that leads to the conclusion; but how can I follow such a line in a depictive work such as a literary novel? The novelist *presents* the truth; they do not construct a line of reasoning that leads to it! Can a concept be transfigured into an image or a figure of speech or some kind of symbol? Can the process of verification be depicted? The philosopher thinks the truth or the proposition. How can the novelist enable us to see it with the eye of the mind? The novelist can communicate the romanticness of the novel by depicting gestures or scenes such as an embrace, a kiss, a look, a smile, a touch, a ramble in the garden, a blush—can ideas be depicted by any of these?" Besides, the critic would add, "the romantic novel may communicate knowledge about the meaning of romanticness by the way the novelist depicts a romantic scene, but the scene we see is particular. It may imply a universal or satisfactory knowledge. If the novelist can communicate philosophical knowledge, in what way is it different from the philosopher's? Again, the philosopher aims at the universal—how can they depict the universal? Finally, philosophical knowledge is apprehended in the medium of concepts, but the knowledge implicit in a literary novel is apprehended in the medium of intuition or feeling. Can a novelist communicate philosophical knowledge and remain a novelist?"

The key to an adequate response to these objections should proceed from an analysis of the following questions. First, what are the aims of the literary novelist, in general, and the philosophical novelist, in particular? I raise this question because the different types of literary genres are distinguished by their themes, and the theme of the novel communicates the kind of knowledge it communicates. Thus, if we know the dynamics of how the literary novel communicates knowledge, we should be able to determine how the philosophical novel communicates philosophical knowledge. Next, what is the aim of the philosophical novelist? Put differently, what type of datum do the philosopher and the novelist reflect on in the process of creating their work? What is the aim of this reflection? The datum of the first is a conceptual framework, and the datum of the second is a depictive framework. Could the aim of both of them be the truth of some aspect of nature or human life?

Second, what makes a novel a literary work of art and a work a philosophical work? I raise this question because my quest is a quest for *literariness and philosophicalness*. I spotlight these two concepts because a philosophical novel is a literary work, but not every literary novel is a philosophical work. Accordingly, the question arises: Can philosophicalness, which defines the essence of philosophical activity or any kind of object, *inhere in the literary dimension of the literary novel?*

First, the aim of the philosopher. Broadly speaking, regardless of whether they are a physicist, a biologist, a sociologist, a psychologist, or an anthropologist, the scientist seeks to know a dimension of the scheme of nature. Natural objects exist as ready-made objects. The defining feature of the scientific method is that scientific knowledge is *attained and verified* by sensuous observation and its extensions, viz., experiments, instruments, and mathematical calculation. Accordingly, scientific knowledge is descriptive in character. Its truth or falsity is determined by direct reference or correspondence with the object of knowledge. If this is the case, and it is, what does the philosopher seek to know? If they seek the truth, what kind of truth do they seek? Most, if not all, the philosophers would agree that *the realm of philosophical knowledge is the realm of values.* The realm of values is the realm of meaning. Values exist as ideals; they are realized in human experience as meaning: the fabric of realized or lived value is meaning. For example, "love" is an ideal. Love in itself does not exist. What exists is different conceptions, different types, and different ways of loving—moral, human, romantic, or filial love, and these different types are practiced differently in different societies and by different individuals.

The scientist strives to uncover the facts of nature, but the philosopher aims to ascertain the meaning of these facts. We may classify human values into three main categories: goodness, beauty, and wisdom. Each category comprises a wide spectrum of subsidiary categories. For example, goodness comprises values such as justice, honesty, friendship, courage, love, and compassion. Beauty comprises values such as grace, elegance, loveliness, comedy, and grandeur. Wisdom comprises values such as prudence, erudition, veracity, candor, soundness, and integrity. Each one of these subsidiary values can also comprise subsidiary values. The preceding set of values is positive because they are desirable or because they are conducive to human happiness. However, each one of them has its opposite or negative; for example, the opposite of goodness is badness, the opposite of beauty is ugliness, and the opposite of wisdom is foolishness. This applies to its subsidiary values. The opposite of each value is disvalue. The realization is that negative values in human life impede human growth and development. Yet, they are an integral part of the enterprise of human living.

The task of the philosopher, ever since the rise of philosophy in the ancient Greek period to the present, has been to explain or understand the meaning of existence, in general, and human existence, in particular. This is the central concern of axiology and metaphysics: Why does the universe exist rather than not? Why do I exist rather than not? How should I live and die as a human being in a non-human nature, one that seems to be indifferent to human purposes and aspirations? Does God exist? Does it make a difference if God exists or does not exist? I do not exaggerate in saying that the major philosophical systems, views, and theories that punctuate the history of philosophy directly or indirectly center on these and related questions. For example, Plato's *Republic* begins with the question of justice: What is justice? The answer to this question necessarily led to an exposition of the basic principles of education, epistemology, metaphysics, art, defense, and religion, in short, the values that are essential to human life. We do not err if we say that the kind of epistemology and metaphysics he constructed was intended to justify the kind of values that should govern the good or just life at the individual and social levels. However, this was also the aim of Hellenistic, modern, and early contemporary philosophy. Consider for a moment a recent philosopher such as Whitehead who followed in the footsteps of Plato, Aristotle, Descartes, Kant, and Hegel—what was the aim of the metaphysical system he expounded in *Process and Reality* but to provide a defensible basis for the existence of the universal in the different domains of life in religion, ethics, art, politics, education, and practical life? How can we live confidently, creatively, hopefully, and courageously if the foundation of this life is not certain, if it is not rationally and morally justifiable?

The metaphysical system, which entails an epistemology and a logic, is a conceptual framework that does not exist as an end in itself; it exists as a means to an end, and the end is the illumination of the nature of the values that govern the different types of activity—moral, artistic, political, social, religious, technological, cultural: How should we understand or interpret these values? For example, what is the purpose of aesthetic theory but to explain the essential nature of the artwork and the aesthetic experience? Furthermore, what makes an artifact art but the values it embodies? Is the artwork not a world of meaning? Again, what is the purpose of ethical theory but to explain the nature of moral values, such as justice, love, or friendship?

It is now time to ask: What is the aim of the literary novelist? I raise this question because the philosophical novel is a literary novel: being a literary work of art is a necessary condition for being a philosophical novel. Accordingly, if the philosophical novel communicates knowledge, it should communicate it as a literary novel. It is generally agreed among aestheticians and literary theorists that the primary aim of the literary novel is to communicate knowledge—an understanding, an insight, a revelation, or an enlightenment of a problem, a question, or an aspect of meaning that relates to human life. I have provided an answer to the question of the aim of the literary novelist in my analysis of the nature of the artwork and the aesthetic experience in the second half of this chapter. I have argued that a literary novel is a story, but not every story is a literary work. A story is art, and, consequently, a literary work, inasmuch as it is a significant form. The texture of this form is *aesthetic qualities*. The realization of these qualities in the aesthetic experience culminates in the creation of what I called an "aesthetic object." Accordingly, every significant form, one that inheres in the created artwork, is a possible aesthetic object.

The philosopher apprehends and articulates this meaning conceptually and propositionally; the literary novelist apprehends and articulates it depictively. This claim is based on the firm assumption that, as an ideal, value is a limitless possibility of realization. It is indeterminate, or formless; yet, it can assume infinite possible forms. This is why, for example, a value such as love can be apprehended and articulated in myriads of musical, literary, dynamic, cultural, pictorial, photographic, and conceptual forms. However, my critic would make an objection to this line of reasoning. The thrust of the objection is that the literary novelist cannot communicate philosophical knowledge or understanding depictively because this kind of knowledge is logical, conceptual, demonstrative, and verifiable. It is not possible to depict a line of reasoning or to establish the falsity or truth of an idea. Two critical remarks here are in order.

First, a philosophical work is a kind of significant form; it is a means to an end, and the end is an understanding of a question or dimension of meaning. When I read Aurelius' *Meditations,* Whitehead's *Process and Reality,* or Russell's *Analysis of Mind,* I intellectually walk through a field of concepts, propositions, assumptions, conceptual analysis, and arguments. My experience in this process is one of seeing and intuiting the kind of meaning the philosopher tries to capture and communicate. As a reader, I aim at the meaning that lurks within or behind this field of propositions, arguments, and analysis. Is the scientific, religious, or ordinary conversation we use not a symbolic form of expression? Does the meaning that inheres in a linguistic formation differ in its ontic status from the aesthetic meaning that inheres in a work of art? Do I not aim at this very meaning when I experience the artistic work, and do I not aim at this kind of meaning when I read a philosophical or scientific text? What I intuit when I read or hear a symbolic expression is meaning, but ontologically, meaning is formless because it does not exist as a physical or psychological object; it exists as a pure moment or drop of pure experience. It does not have an interior or exterior; it does not hide anything from us. We intuit it as a whole, and we intuit it as a spiritual drop of being. The fundamental concern of Dewey in *Art as Experience* is a concern for the ontological status of aesthetic meaning. For example, this meaning emerges as a world when we read a literary novel or when we experience any serious work of art. However, the pursuit of meaning is not the monopoly of the philosopher; it is also the objective of the theologian, the scientist, and the artist in general.

However, if the philosophers' quest is a quest for meaning, what makes a philosophical work *philosophical*? The differentiae that distinguish a philosophical work from any other type of work are the method it employs in (a) intuiting and articulating a content of meaning conceptually and (b) establishing the truth or validity of apprehending and articulating it conceptually. First, the philosopher apprehends meaning in terms of concepts or categories the way the painter apprehends it in terms of lines and colors, the way the dancer apprehends it in terms of motion, or the way the musician apprehends in terms of sound. Second, they try to establish the truth or falsity of their apprehension and articulation by means of analysis, argument, demonstration, and observation. The philosophical mind is logical, analytical, critical; it always thinks and creates in terms of concepts. Again, the philosophical mind is reflective, and the datum of its reflection is the realm of meaning. Like the mind of the scientist who seeks to know the facts that make up the structure of nature by means of sensuous observation, experiments, instruments, inference, and mathematical computation, the philosophical mind seeks to know the meaning of these facts and tries to establish the truth or falsity of their knowledge by means of logical reasoning.

Some philosophers believe that the aim of philosophy is linguistic analysis, viz., the logical and conceptual analysis of the different types of human language—scientific, philosophical, ordinary, religious, political, and artistic language. I think that this approach to the aim of philosophy is painfully narrow, not only because the major philosophers from Plato to the recent past, even the present, have treated linguistic analysis as an ingredient, or a task, of philosophical thinking and creation but especially because an adequate analysis of any type of language *presupposes* a certain view, theory, or understanding of the realm of meaning or a dimension of it. Any language presupposes a dimension of meaning. Moral language presupposes moral values, scientific language presupposes nature, political language presupposes political reality, and aesthetic language presupposes art and the aesthetic experience. Accordingly, the criterion we rely on in evaluating the truth or adequacy of the logical or conceptual analysis of any concepts in any type of language is the extent to which its meaning reflects an adequate intuition of the reality of which it is an articulation. The realm of reality is the realm of philosophical reflection.

The general, yet vague idea that the kind of knowledge or truth the philosopher seeks and tries to communicate is generically different from any other type of knowledge is grossly exaggerated, if not mistaken. The realm of values is the field of their inquiry and reflection. This field is not the privilege of the philosopher or any other inquirer; it is objectively given as the realm of nature is given to the scientist or any seeker of knowledge. The differentiae that distinguish literary, philosophical, theological, or scientific knowledge as kinds of knowledge are (a) the method of apprehending and expressing their intuition of a question, problem, or dimension of the realm of values and (b) the way people use it in the different situations of their practical lives. We should not lose sight of the fact that human values are envisioned as an existential response to basic needs or demands of human nature. Neither the modes of their existence nor the ways they are intuited and realized in experience are engraved in stone. They are always flexible, always amenable to new interpretations and refinements. Is the question of the meaning of human life, of what it means to live and die well in this short life of ours, that figures prominently in Tolstoy's *The Death of Ivan Ilych*, any less profoundly, any less powerfully expressed than it is expressed in Heidegger's *Being and Time* or Unamuno's *The Tragic Sense of Life*? Tolstoy enables us to see, feel, and understand the significance of this question by means of the image he created; Heidegger did the same by means of the conceptual, logical, and coherent analysis of the question of the meaning of human life.

However, my critic would now press on: if a certain type of knowledge is philosophical by virtue of the way it is intuited and expressed, how can the same knowledge be intuited and communicated by other symbolic means of expression? Can the content of meaning that exists in the medium of concept be expressed pictorially? This has been a highly contentious question in both aesthetics and literary theory. I refrain from participating in it only because it is not central to my discussion in this book. However, I would, in view of the preceding discussion, answer this question affirmatively. First, the realm of values does not consist of ready-made realities. At the pre-reflective level, a value is, as I argued earlier, a potentiality that can be realized in different symbolic forms. Still, the critic would add, if a literary novel can portray the meaning and significance of a moral question pictorially, what is the justification for calling it philosophical?

We are justified in calling the novel or the genre philosophical because it communicates knowledge of the type of questions philosophers have been asking since the dawn of Western civilization. This knowledge is a source of inspiration for artists, theologians, leaders in education, politicians, and social reformers. It is extremely difficult for any serious thinker or creator in the major areas of human culture to probe the nature of values without taking these analyses into serious consideration. They have passed the test of rigorous meticulous critical evaluation and verification. Regardless of how they are interpreted or the method by which they are communicated, our understanding of human life always reflects the mark of the philosopher. In fact, the basic map of human values was drawn during the peak of ancient Greek philosophy and remains unchanged to this day. However, although it was conceived by philosophers, although it has endured till the present period, and although it remains a fertile source of insight, still, philosophers do not, as I argued earlier, have a monopoly on the intuition, apprehension, and analysis of values for two reasons.

First, pre-reflectively, and regardless of its kind, value is neither material nor immaterial in character; it is pure possibility. Accordingly, it can be formed by any type of medium—plastic, acoustic, dynamic, or literary. This primordial stratum is, I suggest, not only the source of our intuition of the different types of values and our understanding of them, but it is also the basis of interpreting, translating, and evaluating the different works of art. *Second*, the philosopher's intuition of a value and their attempt to establish the validity of their articulation and analysis of its fabric and relevance to human life is a great service to humanity and merits deep appreciation. However, although philosophers have pioneered the exploration, articulation, and systematization of the realm of values and their role in human life, their analysis is neither final nor complete because our understanding of human nature and its possibilities is neither final nor complete. It is possible for the painter, the novelist, or theologian to delve deep into the vast ocean of values as such and delve deeper, wider, and more profoundly than the philosopher has done. This assertion is based on the assumption that any type of creative mind can reflect on this ocean of values, explore its possibilities, and communicate its intuition in a particular symbolic form. The philosophical mind is one such type of mind.

What matters in the discussion of any aspect of a given value is not only the validity of its conception, its utility, or even clarity of its symbolic expression but especially the *disclosure*, conceptually or pictorially, of the depth, exuberance, and truth of this aspect. It would be a mistake to say that philosophical concept is the best means for this kind of disclosure. Some of the artworks that dot the history of human civilization surpass, in their richness and depth, the philosopher's conception or analysis of some values. Let me illustrate this point by an example familiar to the reader: the Grand Inquisitor scene in Dostoevsky's *The Brothers Karamazov*. I shall return to this scene on the following chapter.

Ever since the rise of the European Renaissance, when *freedom* began to be pursued as the primary goal of the individual and the state, the intelligentsia devoted its supreme attention to the pursuit of this ideal. Revolutions, uprisings, demonstrations, and movements of social reforms in education, the labor market, government, and the family were organized. Philosophers as well as artists endorsed and tried to justify this ideal as well as the intellectual and social movements organized in its support. The banner of freedom was carried into the different institutions of European societies—the school, law, family, the workplace, church, art, and government. "Freedom" became the catchword in politics, economics, education, religion, art, and culture. This banner was not carried without a good reason: *It was initiated and pursued in the name of human dignity!* People had been living more as members of a herd than as individuals in a human community. It became clear to all the intellectuals that human dignity is a necessary condition for living with respect, respect for the human being as a human individual. A critical observer of this phenomenon would, I think, wonder, if not question, whether this value expresses an essential demand of human nature and, more concretely, whether it is a worthwhile *existential objective* or even a primary concern of the masses that make up the numberless humanity that populate the earth. It is one thing to talk about lived humanity, but it is something else to talk about ideal humanity. The analysis of human nature by the philosopher or its delineation by the artist is quite different from the humanity that thrives in the sphere of reality.

Accordingly, the question we should ask is, *do people truly want freedom?* Do they give a hoot about human dignity? Is freedom an essential demand of lived humanity? Philosophers have answered these questions affirmatively, and they have advanced countless analyses and arguments in support of their answers. Hardly anyone among the philosophical elite did or would contradict them. And yet, a novelist like Dostoevsky did, and he did it not by the power of persuasive argument but by the power of luminous metaphor, by enabling the reader to see, to feel, and to understand a vitally important truth of *lived humanity*.

The troubling question is not whether freedom is a right founded in a basic demand of human nature but the responsibility it entails: Can I be free if I cannot be responsible for the consequences of my action or the kind of life I live? Is such a freedom a burden? I raise this question because humanity is embedded in nature in two ways; first, our individual humanity is embedded in our bodies, which are parts of nature and, second, human life at the communal and individual levels is anchored in nature. How can the human being be free in this twofold relation to nature? What does it mean to be free? Can I be free if I am a pulse in the cosmic process? Can I be free if I am a moment in the process of history, and if history is a moment in the cosmic process? How can people be free from the shackles of nature, disease, ignorance, poverty, human evil, and especially mortality, all of which seem to be permanent? Is survival not the primary impulse in human nature? Again, how can people be free if they are born as a problem for themselves? Alas, can they be free if their stomachs are empty, if there is no roof over their heads, if they cannot lead a secure, peaceful life? Moreover, they are not born as ready-made realities but as realities to be made, that is, created. They need a lifetime, and maybe several lifetimes to create it, but the moment they are about to create it they stand near their graves. Still, how should they create themselves? How can they realize their life project if they live in a harsh, adverse social environment? However, the confusing question is this: Why should they strive for noble ideals if they know that they will transition into oblivion? Should we take the social scientist seriously when they say, "Create the right environment, you create the right individual?" It may seem that this dictum was created in the minds of some silly idealists!

It seems that the burden of freedom and responsibility is foisted upon the mass of human beings by some malignant cosmic force: Have we chosen our existence or the kind of beings we are? How can we be free if we are not the source of our being? The dramatic aspect of this predicament intensifies when we realize that the structure of the human predicament is not much different today from the way it was during the time of Jesus. This continuity is, I think, what inclined Dostoevsky to probe its depth, intricacy, vagueness, and vital importance with regard to any explanation of the meaning of human life. The rock bed of this condition is a question that provokes, challenges, and glares in the face of any serious-minded human being: *How can I exist as a genuine human being if I am not free, and how can I be free in a world that undermines the possibility of this freedom?*

Like the idealists and the philosophers, Jesus saw that "man does not live by bread alone" and that, regardless of the power that underlies his creation or emergence on the scene of reality, he does not exist in vain; he exists in order to become the human being he should be: humanity is intrinsically valuable. It cannot be violated or undermined. Freedom is, as I have just pointed out, a necessary condition of dignity. People live under the conditions of dignity when they live as human beings, and they live as humans when they live under the conditions of freedom. Is this too much to ask? The answer to this question is painfully difficult because the idealists and the philosophers are correct, and the masses and the pessimists are equally correct. Leading a genuine human life is possible, but it is exclusive of the enlightened elite, and leading a life of the herd is possible—indeed it is a fact. The masses killed Jesus 2000 years ago, and the elite that believed in his message did not save him.

Was Jesus a tragic hero? I tend to think that the Jesus Dostoevsky tried to represent in the Grand Inquisitor scene in *The Brothers Karamazov* is a tragic hero, one who was willing to sacrifice his life for a universal truth, a truth that defines the meaning and destiny of human life, a truth that reveals the impossibility of the possible, a truth that reveals the contradictory nature of human existence, a truth the defies the gods and deifies the human, a truth that reveals the rebellious nature of human nature—that it is an ongoing rebellion against this very contradiction. Did Jesus not know that the masses did not give a hoot about freedom and that only a few were destined to pursue it successfully? Would he have willingly died had he not known in the depth of his mind that humanity is worth dying for, that it does not exist in vain, that a life that does not flourish under the conditions of freedom is not worth living? And yet, he spent the last three years of his life among the masses trying to liberate them from the dark cave in which they were living with the full knowledge that they were not interested in his kingdom of light, that they would not hesitate to kill him if they had to. In fact, he gave them gems of wisdom, he healed many of their physical and psychological wounds, he walked among them as an angel of peace, he even performed miracles for them, and yet, they killed Him! Jesus could have saved himself, but he did not. He lived and died for an ideal.

However, this is not all. The dramatic aspect of Jesus' visit to Seville, which culminated in his encounter with the Grand Inquisitor and reached its acme in that inscrutable kiss on the lips of the cardinal, revealed the tragic character of Jesus. The cardinal knew that he was a ray of divine light, and Jesus knew that he was condemned to death. Still, he kissed him, and his kiss was a kiss of love. Did that kiss signify the power of the human ideal, of the deep-seated desire to aspire for the human in us? In that encounter, we existentially see, feel, and understand that the Jesus who was rejected and crucified 2000 years ago was again rejected and was condemned to death 700 years later.

The Grand Inquisitor scene captures in a most vivid, exuberant, and dramatic way the paradoxical, tragic, and ironic truth inherent in the quest for freedom as a realistically possible ideal. Dostoevsky did not reveal this truth through a long and intricate line of reasoning but by depicting and disclosing the ironic, paradoxical, and tragic fate inherent in the quest for freedom as a viable ideal. He did this by inviting Jesus to pay a visit to the city of Seville in Spain during the Inquisition. A crowd had been carrying the coffin of a dead young girl on its way to the cemetery when they recognized him. Jesus was waiting at the portal of the cathedral when the crowd was moving in. The coffin was opened. Jesus resurrected the young girl, as he did in the past! The crowd witnessed the miracle and knew it was he—Jesus. Yes, he had come back, as he said he would!

In the meantime, the Cardinal, who had been watching the scene, recognized him too. He disliked what he saw. In his quiet, magisterial way, he ordered the arrest and trial of the son of God! Jesus was sentenced to death. The Cardinal paid him a visit in his prison cell. They had an intense, moving conversation in which Jesus remained silent and the Cardinal spoke to the silent Jesus. He informed him that the masses were not interested in his ideals, values, miracles, or kingdom; in short, they were not interested in freedom. They were interested in survival and a few crumbs of pleasure. They were not ready to carry the cross of freedom and responsibility on their backs! He accused Jesus of disturbing the peace and interfering in managing the lives of his flock. "Yes," my critic would now ask, "but how did Dostoevsky delineate the truth that the masses do not want to carry the cross of freedom and responsibility? Did he communicate it by the conversation that took place between the speaking Cardinal and the silent Jesus?"

Not at all! He depicted this truth in and through the scene in which Jesus joined the crowd and resurrected the young girl and through the subsequent scene with the Cardinal. This scene is not merely a descriptive narrative but a luminous image in which we see, feel, and comprehend this truth by the *way* the crowd received Jesus, by *the way* they knew he was the real Jesus, by *the way* the Cardinal treated him, by *the way* they had a lopsided conversation, and especially by *the way* that kiss of love was another *miracle*! The moment we begin to read the scene aesthetically we discover that the story Dostoevsky wrote is a mosaic of aesthetic qualities; we also discover that metaphor, which veils a simile, is the prominent figure of speech in this story. First, the figure of the Grand Inquisitor embodies the character of Satan: he is Satan, the highest exemplification of evil. He wears a human body dressed in the robe of a Grand Inquisitor. He represents the force of evil—of lust for power, hate, vengeance, oppression, envy, destruction, and bigotry. Second, the figure of Jesus embodies the character of the historical Jesus. He is Jesus, the highest exemplification of goodness—of freedom, love, courage, honesty, justice, and the love of freedom. The confrontation between these two characters is a confrontation between good and evil. Although the Grand Inquisitor condemns Jesus to death, the way the historical Jesus was condemned to death, Jesus triumphs by the power of the kiss of love the way he triumphed over death on the cross. Oh, how enigmatic was that kiss!

The deeper we charge into the aesthetic world of this scene, the farther we move from the scene as a story, the closer we move to the world entailed by the conflict between Satan and Jesus, Good and Evil, the deeper we move into the world entailed by the question of the meaning of human life and destiny. However, this move does not allow us to abandon the world depicted by Dostoevsky. On the contrary, the deeper we move into this world of meaning, the more the aesthetic dimension of this story expands.

The larger world that unfolds in our imagination is not conceptual, though it involves concepts. It exists to my imagination as a vista, *as presence*—a luminous presence. I see this emerging world in the figures of Jesus and the Cardinal as they act and interact with each other. I see good and evil shining from them, I see humanity emanating from this scene, I see myself in this scene, I see myself as an actor in it. However, this kind of seeing is also an activity of discovering; I discover that I am the author of this drama, and I discover that I am a witness to what I discover. This kind of experience, as well as this kind of seeing, is one of the highest modes of knowing, of knowing what the philosopher seeks to know and communicate in their own way. Nevertheless, unlike the knowledge the philosopher communicates, which is abstract, this kind of knowledge is existential and transformative because I am completely involved in discovering and constructing it! It is founded not only in seeing it and feeling it but especially in creating it.

I shall continue this discussion in the following chapter.

References and Suggested Bibliography

Mitias, Michael. (1987). *What Makes an Experience Aesthetic?* Rodopi; *The Possibility of Aesthetic Experience*. Amsterdam: *Kluwer, 1987; Aesthetic Quality and Aesthetic Experience*. Amsterdam: Rodopi, 1988; *The Philosopher and the Devil*, London: Olympia, 2018.

CHAPTER 5

Analysis of Two Metaphors

Introduction

My loyal yet relentless critic would now wonder: "I understand the line of reasoning you have so far advanced in support of your claim that, first, in the sphere of the literary novel, possession of aesthetic qualities is the principle of literary distinction, second, the theme is the principle of genre distinction, third, as the theme of the literary novel can be philosophical in nature, the philosophical novel can, and should, be treated as a literary genre, and, fourth, like all literary works, the philosophical novel is, by its very nature, cognitive and that the kind of knowledge it communicates is philosophical. The structure of your argument is clear to me, but the exact meaning and validity of the fourth proposition are not. I cannot discern the validity of this proposition if its meaning is not clear: How can philosophicalness inhere in the literary stratum of the novel? As you can see, I am keenly interested in whether a literary novel can be philosophical, and if it can, *how* it can communicate knowledge. In the preceding chapter, you argued that metaphor is the vehicle of communicating knowledge, but you did not explain how it can do this. If philosophical knowledge can inhere in a literary novel, it should undergo a change of identity from being *conceptual* to being *aspectual* or qualitative in character. Can we call a type of knowledge philosophical if it loses its conceptual character? Moreover, a literary novel is essentially a depictive work of art. As you cogently argued in Chap. 2, the mere presence of a philosophical discourse or meditation in a novel does not necessarily make it philosophical. The novel should declare its philosophicalness as a literary work of art. There is a big difference between containing and embodying. The philosophical novel does not contain its aesthetic qualities as given elements; it embodies them. They inhere in it as potentialities. The novel as a whole is philosophical, not merely this or that element of it. This is why the mere inclusion of a philosophical element does not necessarily make it philosophical. Accordingly, if a central element of the novel, for example, the main character, is philosophical, then every one of its parts should necessarily exist for the sake of the philosophicalness of this character. If this happens, the philosophicalness of this character would radiate through every scene, conversation, action, or incident of the novel. The reader would experience its philosophicalness as an essential aspect of the novel. Accordingly, the aesthetic object that comes to life in the aesthetic experience would be imbued with philosophicalness the way a living organism would be imbued with life. Thus, an aesthetic object would exist to the reader as a presence, *a luminous presence*, one the reader sees, feels, and understands directly without the mediation of any concepts or propositions. It may or may not be possible for this presence to be richer or poorer, more or less truthful, more or less illuminating than the meaning communicated by a philosopher. Nevertheless, the meaning the reader apprehends would be genuinely *philosophical*. Do I understand your view adequately?"

"Yes, you do."

"Then, would you shed another ray of light on the conception of metaphor you used in your analysis of the metaphorical character of Prince Myshkin in *The Idiot* and Jesus and the Cardinal in the *The Grand Inquisitor* scene of in Dostoevsky's *The Brothers Karamazov*? What element or what about the metaphor enables it to be a vehicle of knowledge? A vehicle is carrier, a transmitter of a certain content, which may or may not be material in character. For example, the phonic structure of a word is treated by most philosophers and linguists as a "shell" or "vehicle" that contains meaning, but a metaphor is not a word; it is a special kind of linguistic organization, viz., a figure of speech. If a metaphor is such a figure, the question arises: How does this kind of figure of speech function as a vehicle of knowledge? By what magic does the novelist transform the identity of a philosophical concept into a kind of reality that exists as a quality in a metaphorical context so that the magical transformation that happens in this type of creative expression is one in which the philosophicalness that exists as the unity of aesthetic qualities is now experienced as a philosophical content?

The Concept of Metaphor

An answer to this question should, I think, begin with an analysis of the concept of metaphor and the kind of linguistic structure that makes it a metaphor. This claim is based on the assumption that if a metaphor is a vehicle of knowledge, then one of its elements, or something about it, should enable it to function as a transmitter of knowledge. Thus, we should begin the analysis with a general concept of metaphor. I resort to this kind of beginning because the concept of metaphor has a long history of development and application. My aim in this section is neither to propose a theory of metaphor nor to defend or critically evaluate a certain theory in the realm of literature or philosophy but to advance a concept of the *ontic structure of* this figure of speech because this structure implies the conditions under which metaphor communicates knowledge: How can we say that metaphor is a vehicle of knowledge, and how can we analyze a type of metaphorical discourse, be it a sentence, a phrase, a poem, a novel, or a philosophical work, if we do not assume a certain concept, at least an understanding, of the kind of metaphorical structure and the way it functions as a basis of our analysis? Indeed, the more adequate our concert or understanding of this concept, the more adequate our analysis will be. However, how can our concept of metaphor be adequate if we do not comprehend the *ontic structure* that underlies its scope and application? By "ontic structure," I mean "the way" its essential, constitutive elements are organized into a coherent whole. It is "ontic" because it is indispensable for the being of the metaphor or because it is the *source* of its being as this kind of figure of speech.

Well, how can we arrive at a concept of the ontic structure of the metaphor, one that explains adequately how it can be a vehicle of philosophical knowledge? We may arrive at it by the method of abstraction, that is, by observing the basic elements that are common to all metaphorical forms and articulating them into a concept that expresses the structure we are seeking. However, it would be wise to avoid this method only because it will necessarily involve us in an extensive inquiry into a multitude of theories and conceptions, which is beyond this scope of this book. A more feasible, effective, and, I think, generally acceptable way of arriving at the ontic structure of metaphor is to analyze the first statement of the concept of the metaphor that was advanced by Aristotle and which has been the mainspring of theorization on this concept during the past 600 years. Besides, Aristotle arrived at his theory of metaphor by extensively examining this figure of speech in the different forms of ancient Greek literature in poetry, drama, novel, and prose. Hardly any contemporary literary theorist would either undervalue or deny the relevance of his insight to the analysis of the concept of the metaphor, not because it is complete or perfect, for it is not, but because his concept, which defines the structure of metaphor, remains *sound* to this day. This definition is my primary concern in this study.

Aristotle's Concept of Metaphor

Broadly speaking, for Aristotle, a metaphor is a vehicle of discovering new ideas, that is, of communicating ideas we did not know before. How does this form of linguistic expression communicate new ideas? Aristotle answers this question by analyzing the structural elements of metaphor and the way these elements are interrelated. "Metaphor," he writes, "is the application of an alien name by transference either from genus to species, from species to genus, from species to species, or by analogy, that is, proportion" (Aristotle 2005, 1475b, 7–8). The key words in this account are "transfer," "analogy," and "proportion." "Transfer" signifies a cognitive turn, or movement, from one word, or idea, to another word, for metaphor is basically composed of two constitutive elements. This movement is necessary by virtue of the structure of the metaphor. It is made possible by the fact that it is an assertion. This linguistic form is, by its very structure, directive, in which the subject points to its referent, that is, the referent is about the subject. When I say "The fire is dying," my hearer knows what a fire is, but they do not know whether it is dying. This is why the mere pronouncement of "fire" directly inclines the hearer to move their attention from "fire" to "dying." In the example Aristotle gives, namely, "There lies my ship," the movement is made from genus to species. It is necessary because "lie" qualifies the ship. Here the meaning of "lie" is implicitly transferred to the ship instead of "anchor," which is normally applied to ships when they are moored in a certain place. Thus, instead of saying "There anchors my ship," the speaker said, "There lies my ship." The replacement of "anchor" with "lie" transforms the sentence into a metaphor because the new idea, that is, "lie," is wider and richer than the idea "anchor," which is reserved for ships when they are moored in a certain place. When the ship is qualified with "lie," it is not deprived of the quality, or capacity, of being anchored in a certain place; it retains it and acquires the quality of "lie"; that is, we think, or conceive, it as being anchored in a certain way, not merely as motionless in a certain place, for example, the way human beings lie in bed or on a sofa, a position peculiar to animals and people. This example is based on a hidden or suppressed simile. "There lies my ship" can be read as my ship lies there like a human being lies in bed or on a sofa in a certain way, which may be described depictively or poetically.

For Aristotle, the basis of metaphor is simile. This is why he treats a simile as a metaphor. "Analogy or portion," he says immediately following his explanation of how the cognitive turn occurs from species to genus and species to species, is "when the second term is to the first as the fourth to the third. We may then use the fourth for the second or the second for the fourth. Sometimes too we qualify the metaphor by adding the term to which the proper word is relative" (Aristotle 2005, 1475b, 16–19). The basis of this form of metaphor is the similarity of certain features between two terms. For example, we can say "Evening is the old age of the day" or "Old age is the evening of life." In both metaphorical statements, "evening" signifies "end," the "gradual departure or vanishing" of a day or the life of a human being—a kind of death. This kind of metaphor is informative because when we qualify the end of the life of a human being with "evening," we not only spotlight its cessation, or end, but also the possible ideas of darkness, ghastliness, fear, uncertainty, and countless ways of trying to imagine the world of darkness that awaits people. This type of imagining is entailed by the idea of evening. When the transfer from the subject to the qualifier happens to be brilliant, the metaphor acquires a special aesthetic quality: "The similes of the poets do the same, and therefore, if they are good similes, they give an effect of brilliance. The simile, as has been said before, is a metaphor, differing from it only in the way it is put" (Aristotle 2005, 1410b, 16–19). However, although it can be aesthetic in character, the main function of the metaphor is communication of new ideas.

Regardless of whether it is an allegory, parable, story, fable, hyperbole, metonymy, antithesis, a metaphor is essentially a simile, that is, a relation between two terms that share some basic similarities. These similarities are the basis of the metaphorical relation. The first term is subject, ground, or bearer, and the second is the vehicle or target. The first is stated, and the second is intended. The first is ordinary, or lexical, and the second is stranger or unexpected. However, the two terms are similar in certain respects or in some ways. In some cases, the similarity is indicated by terms such as "as," "like," or similar modifiers. The point Aristotle emphasizes is that the target, or vehicle, suggests that it is a "carrier," one that communicates ideas. The reader of the metaphor is not usually interested in the subject because they know its signification. They are interested in the vehicle because it is a bearer of new ideas. "People are not much taken either by obvious arguments (using the word 'obvious' to mean what is plain to everybody and needs no investigation), nor by those which puzzle us when we hear them stated, but only by those which convey their information to us as soon as we hear them, provided that we had not the information already; or which the mind only just fails to keep us with" (Aristotle 2005, 1418b, 23–26).

The use of metaphor is not restricted to poetry or literature in general; it is also used effectively in the field of philosophy. It is used as a means of not merely clarifying the meaning of recalcitrant concepts but also establishing the validity of certain propositions or arguments, primarily because metaphor can disclose the meaning of an idea in the fullness of its truth so that one can comprehend it immediately. It is this kind of disclosure, which we intuit directly, that "so far as the meaning of what is said is concerned, make an argument acceptable" (Aristotle, 1410b, 27–29). As an example, consider for a moment Plato's allegory of the cave.

The Allegory of the Cave

What if we posit to Plato and the other philosophers who lived before and contemporaneous to him that truth, in the sense of tested knowledge, exists and that the attainment of this truth is critically important for human happiness and progress at the social and individual level, a goal every cultivated being would desire and seek as a supreme good, that a genuine comprehension of the truth, implicit in the different types of knowledge, is founded in the intuition of an ultimate reality whose being is the source and foundation of all reality, that most, if not all, human beings are ignorant and lead a sheep-like life and have no clear notion of what it means for a person to be a human being, that a morally, intellectually, aesthetically, and politically enlightened human being, one who feels a moral obligation to liberate those people from the shackles of ignorance, has a vision of the ultimate reality and knows its importance, that this person has decided to construct a system of education designed to enable the people who dwell in the world of ignorance to leave this world and have, by means of an effective course of instruction, a vision of the ultimate reality—yes, suppose we posit these assumptions, which we may also call "propositions," what steps should this course of instruction consists of? Or, suppose an angel from the heaven of knowledge were to visit these people, how would such an angel describe the state of this society and recommend a method of liberating them from their ignorance?

However, regardless of whether such an angel descends from the heaven of knowledge and discovers the predicament of these people, we can ask, what is the aim, or aims, of education, one that seeks the truth of human and natural reality? How can we design our social and individual life-projects if they are not based on a genuine understanding of the purpose of existence in general and human existence in particular? For example, should we not take into serious consideration the fact that reality is constantly changing and that everything that exists will sooner or later cease to exist? Again, can our knowledge of nature be true or adequate if we do not comprehend the source or power that underlies it? Can we design an adequate system of education if we do not proceed in this task from a genuine understanding of human nature? These and similar questions prompted Plato to construct the allegory of the cave. This allegory revolves around people who live in a cave and are chained to one of its walls. They cannot move, and they cannot look sideways. They face a blank wall. A fire burns on a parapet over their head behind them. Behind the fire, some people carrying different types of toys are moving in different directions creating different types of shadows on the wall in front of the prisoners. The shadows are all they see and all they know.

One of the prisoners is freed from his chains. He moves around. Eventually, he discovers the real identity of the cave—the fire, the parapet, the toys, the people who were carrying the toys that were casting shadows on the wall, in short, the real predicament he and his fellow prisoners are in. He discovers this predicament with some difficulty, but he discovers it. Now he knows that the world in which he lived is not real. But then, he leaves the cave through a door on one side of the cave. He finds himself in the world of nature. He moves around and gradually discovers the real objects that make up the structure of the real world—so far. Moreover, he discovers the basic universals and principles of mathematics and geometry. This discovery is also not easy. It takes time and serious intellectual effort. Finally, he looks upward. He looks at the sun. He gazes at it. At first, his eyes are blinded, but in time, he is able to focus his attention on it and reflects on its nature and relation to Earth. He discovers that its light is the source of life on earth; he also discovers that it is the source of all-natural reality, for if its light ceases to exist, natural reality collapses into nothing. He finally discovers that the sun is the true reality.

As a narrative, this allegory is composed of two images: the image of the cave and that of the sun. They constitute the ontic structure of the allegory *qua* metaphor. They are the bases of two journeys—the first is from the dark cave to the physical sun, and the second is from the world of ignorance to the world of knowledge. Darkness stands for ignorance and the sun for true knowledge. The journey of the freed prisoner in the cave, which represents the journey of the philosopher from ordinary knowledge to wisdom, or the journey of any seeker of true knowledge, is practically a journey from ignorance to knowledge. By "ignorance," Plato means "absence of knowledge." Moreover, the image of the sun stands for the source and ground of reality, and the image of the cave stands for the world of nature, which is a world of "appearance," primarily because it is a world of constant change. Plato refers to the source and ground of all reality as The Good. Accordingly, The Sun and The Good constitute the ontic structure of the metaphor: The Sun is The Good. "The Sun" is its ground or subject, and the Good is its vehicle or bearer. Here, the transfer is from species to genus; it is based on a hidden or suppressed simile. It implies that "The Good" is like "The Sun" because, like the sun, which is the source and the ground of physical reality, The Good is the source and ground of all reality, including the reality of the physical sun. As a genus, the connotation of "The Good" is infinitely richer than that of the physical sun. Thus, a person who reads *The Republic* that culminates in the analysis of the "Divided Line" and then the allegory of the cave would necessarily move from the apprehension of the idea of the physical sun to that of The Good because the concept of the physical sun is familiar, while that of The Good is not.

Plato did not start *The Republic* with a discussion of the allegory of the cave. The discussion of the allegory comes after he discusses the basic institutions of the state and his theory of knowledge and metaphysics. The allegory presupposes this discussion. This is why, although very briefly, I began my analysis of the allegory of the cave *qua* metaphor with a series of reflections on the signification, implications, and importance of the knowledge of The Good as a necessary condition for creating an adequate vision of the kind of education that aims at (a) the liberation of people from ignorance and (b) the establishment of a good society.

The Grand Inquisitor Scene

We may view the analysis of the allegory of the cave in the preceding section, which represents an important use of metaphor in philosophy, as an introduction to a discussion of its centrality in the realm of literature in general and the philosophical novel in particular. One of the main advantages of Aristotle's conception of metaphor is that it spotlights the ontic structure of this figure of speech. I only hope that it shed a ray of understanding on the logical dynamics of this structure.

I think it is now appropriate to analyze in some detail *The Grand Inquisitor* scene in Dostoevsky's *The Brothers Karamazov*. As I did in my analysis of the allegory of the cave, I shall begin with some reflections on the theme of this scene. It is rather complex, but I am confident that my reflections will illuminate its ontic structure as a metaphor and, more concretely, its vehicle as a means of communicating knowledge. I have called my remarks "reflections" because they do not constitute a logical or coherent discourse but interrelated ideas that point to the scope of the vehicle of the metaphor. I do this because this scope is wide and suggestive by its very nature.

Reflections Under what conditions can people lead a life true to their humanity, that is, to the values that express the essential needs or demands that arise from the human essence? This question, which figures prominently in the work of the major philosophers, theologians, social scientists, and social critics, implies that leading a life true to our humanity is not only an obligation but also the purpose for which people exist. Accordingly, leading this kind of life is *human destiny*. Every human being deserves to pursue this destiny. However, what does it mean to lead a life true to our humanity? What is the feature, capacity, or aspect that defines the human essence? I may be told that the essential capacities that constitute the human essence are thinking, feeling, and willing. The first aims at knowledge, the second aims at love and beauty, and the third aims at the realization of the creative urge in people as human individuals. When we lead a life in which we grow in knowledge, love, appreciation of beauty, and pursue a creative endeavor, we lead a life true to our humanity. However, the question I raised at the beginning of this paragraph asks for the conditions under which one can lead such a life. Suppose we create a robot that seeks knowledge, feels love, appreciates beauty, and functions as a creative machine, would it be possible to say that it leads a life true to the human essence? No, because it is a robot, that is, because its life is programmed by a power external to it, because its life does not originate from its mind, heart, and will. A robot cannot truly say and cannot comprehend the meaning of "I," "my," and "mine." It may experience or feel pleasure, pain, loneliness, sadness, or thrill, and it may exhibit symptoms of these types of "experiences," but it does not comprehend what it means to experience them, primarily because they are acquired or programmed into its functioning mechanism.

A necessary condition for leading a life true to our humanity is freedom. "Freedom?" My critic would exclaim. But what is freedom? Is it merely the capacity to make choices? Is it doing whatever one happens to feel or desire without any type of constriction? No. First, the idea of choice implies action; it is a choice of a particular action. Inability to act on it nullifies the choice; it renders the choice a mere desire or feeling. Second, a choice that is not based on a rational or moral principle is a loose, fitful, random, or capricious selection. Again, how can I be free if I am sick, ignorant, disenfranchised, or oppressed? How can I be free if I am not given the opportunity to design my life-project and pursue it with all my mind, heart, will, if my capacities of knowledge, feeling, and willing, loving and my capacity to appreciate beauty and choose my vocation do not function according to my vision of my life-project? It would seem that freedom is not merely the capacity to make choices but *to realize ourselves as human individuals*—to know our human and individual identities and live according to this knowledge.

But, do people want to be free? Except for a few who are truly cultivated or enlightened, a great majority of people do not want freedom. They are satisfied with a very modest measure of freedom, enough to keep them living. They are more interested in satisfying their stomachs, sexual desires, a semblance of social existence, physical, and psychological, and social security, and a few morsels of pleasure than in striving for freedom and the essential demands it entails. We may say that the human in us exists as a potentiality and that the realization of this potentiality in an unfriendly nature and most of the time unfriendly society requires courage, understanding, power, perseverance, dedication, willingness to suffer much pain, and readiness to sacrifice one's comfortable, easy-going way of life. Not many people are willing to sacrifice their comfortable way of life to one of struggle, frustration, constant stress, and frequently insurmountable challenges, especially if we take into consideration the fact that human life is short. Besides, it is possible that there is an urge in human nature that cries for self-realization or self-fulfillment, but is it not possible to say that people are lazy by nature? Cast a quick look at the way people understand happiness and seek it and focus your attention on the existential conditions of human life. What makes people content and happy? What do they actually want? What is their dream in life—a home, a nice car, financial security, a job, a few drops of entertainment, some sexual pleasure, some social recognition? How many people truly seek and enjoy serious music, drama, architecture, literature, dance, or sculpture? How many desire to read the books of scientists and historians or the confessions of the artists, mystics, and monks? How many people give some of their time to the sick, the lonely, the poor, the oppressed, or to those in prison? How many people honor true friendship? How many people feel the real presence of God when they go to church, the temple, or the mosque? What if all people do all of these things, at least in principle? What would our life be like then?

This last question casts a ray of doubt on the claim that leading a life true to our humanity is human destiny or that freedom is a necessary condition for leading such a life. It may seem that freedom is a far-fetched dream. First, we are integral parts of nature; our bodies cannot deviate one whit from its laws. These laws, as well as the events that make up the fabric of nature, are indifferent to human needs, desires, or wellbeing. Human begins can conceive or imagine noble, beautiful, and genuine ways of human living and they may justify these ways rationally and morally. However, we should remember that any type of justification we give to our ways of life is a form of human creation—it is anthropocentric.

However, in whatever they think or do, people are subject to the laws of nature. What is worse for them is that they do not choose to be born; they discover themselves as existing in a certain place, society, time, and in a certain family. They also discover that they are no more than pulses, moments, in the cosmic process. Still worse is that they discover that their life is short. Why did they happen to exist? As Shakespeare insightfully remarked, they are actors on the world stage; they enter it through one door and leave it through another door most of the time without asking or knowing why they are chosen for the role they play on that stage. But, alas, are they chosen for the role they play? Who chooses them to play that role? The tragic predicament of human beings is that their lives are vitiated by hardships, disease, war, conflict, ignorance, hate, natural disasters, fear, uncertainty, and selfishness, in short, human and natural evil. And yet, they have to suffer and live—why? Do you doubt this brief characterization? Ask any human being who reaches the last station of their life or who stands on the edge that overlooks the infinite ocean of nothingness: What was it about? Are we really passing moments in the cosmic process? Alas! Are we destined to lead a life of toil in a prison called "the cosmic process"? Shakespeare said that we are actors on the world stage. However, how can we be actors if we do not choose our existence or the role we are supposed to play? Is it not more accurate to say that we are prisoners in the cosmic process? But, are we? Suppose we are not, the question remains: Regardless of whether we are actors or prisoners, why should we exist? Can we be liberated from this painful predicament? Do you blame people if they choose the easy way of life and forget about freedom? The few who lead a life of freedom may live with the illusion that their existence is justified, but what about the masses of humanity that are not able to think about this or any other type of illusion? Should they live and die in ignorance? If ignorance is bliss, as the "they" say, what is the difference between a person who lives a life true to the human essence, assuming that they achieve it in the middle if not the end of their life, and a person who lives the life of a sheep in a herd of sheep to the very end—what if a member of the herd leaves its herd and confronts a person who lives a life of freedom: "Why do you want to be free?"

"I want to be free because I want to live a life true to my essence."
"Why?"
"This is my destiny."
"By whose law, command, or decree?"
"By the power that created me."
"Did this power ordain that you should suffer in order to be your human self, if you can be yourself? Has it occurred to you that being yourself entails that you, and you alone, are responsible for designing the plan of your individual self and realizing this plan and the kind of life you live? What if you fumble—do you send yourself to a hell of your own making? Did you consider that freedom entails responsibility and that this responsibility is not a privilege but a burden? Is your life of freedom, which you glorify, a life of ongoing burden? Why should you suffer the pangs of this burden when you know that very soon, you shall end up in the realm of eternal oblivion?"

Maybe, but we should look at this question, indeed, at the human predicament that I have already spotlighted very briefly, from the standpoint of Jesus of Nazareth who preached that human beings are destined to freedom, that freedom consists in leading a life true to our humanity, that the source and foundation of this humanity is God, and that the laws and values that should steer this life are the ones revealed in the life of Jesus. They who believe in the divinity of the Son can be saved from the unjustifiable suffering that plagues the human condition—from its transience, uncertainty, and especially from the realization that one can hardly enjoy freedom, which seems to be a far-fetched aspiration in this world.

THE PARABLE OF THE GRAND INQUISITOR

This parable is delivered as a "poem" by Ivan, one of the main characters of *The Brothers Karamazov*. He believes that a caring, loving God, one who feels concern for human beings, responds to their prayers, and will sooner or later save them from suffering and transience in this world, does not exist. If God exists, he would not act the way human beings do. A metaphysical God, a kind of Primary Cause, Unmoved Mover, or The One may or may not exist, but God the Father does not exist.

In the conversation between the brothers, Ivan recites a "poem," which is a parable, in which he describes a visit by Jesus of Nazareth to the city of Seville in Spain in the seventeenth century. It happened that a crowd of people carrying the coffin of a young girl was approaching the entrance of the Cathedral when Jesus appeared at the entrance. The crowd recognized him. How could they miss the visage of the man they had been worshipping and waiting for? He performed two miracles: he healed a blind man and resurrected a young girl from the dead. Who could heal the blind or resurrect people from the dead but Jesus? The crowd was amazed and delighted. Who would not be amazed and delighted at witnessing a miracle, and especially, one performed by the Son of God?

Well, this scene did not escape the eyes of the Grand Inquisitor. He watched Jesus perform the miracles and observed the crowd's reaction to his presence and actions. He did not like what he saw. He ordered Jesus' immediate arrest and execution on the following day. He also ordered the crowd to leave the scene. They obeyed the Inquisitor and abandoned the Son of God, the same Son they had been worshipping every Sunday morning, the same Son they had been waiting for, the same Son who had created Heaven and Earth.

That night, the Grand inquisitor visited Jesus in his prison cell. He had a long conversation with him, but strangely, the conversation was one-sided. The Inquisitor spoke, but Jesus was silent the entire conversation. We may characterize this conversation as an encounter, or duel, between

Jesus and the Devil. It represents the Devil's attempts to tempt Jesus in the desert 700 years ago. The Devil tried to seduce him using three temptations, urging him to perform the following acts: change stone to bread, govern the world, and cast himself out of the temple and be saved by the angels. Jesus refused these temptations, and the Inquisitor knew that he would refuse them again. Why?

Jesus was interested in the world of goodness, of freedom of love, human perfection, justice, authenticity, of a life that radiates from the human spark, the spark that emanates from the divine as such. He offered himself as a sacrifice on the cross for the sake of these values. On the other hand, the Inquisitor viewed himself as the shepherd of the majority of humankind. He espoused the values of the Devil; he accepted the glory of this world rather than the fictional world of love and goodness, viz., freedom. The argument he presented in this one-sided conversation with Jesus that night is that few people are willing to be free; the majority do not want freedom and the burden it entails. They simply want to live a comfortable and pleasant life. Why should anyone like Jesus come to Seville to complicate their lives with an impossible ideal? Why should he disturb the public peace in the City of Man? Why not stay in the City of God where he belongs? I can adumbrate his argument in this way: "You came to Palestine seventeen hundred years ago. A great majority of people were happy with their lot. You tried to convince them that love is the source of happiness on earth and, later on, in the Kingdom of Heaven, but you were not certain of this. You—yes, you—valued love more than anything in the City of Man and thought that it was the source of salvation and eternal happiness. You performed miracles, the way you did today, but the people did not believe you. You wanted to change their way of life, but they did not. You did not even notice that they wanted your miracles but not your love or your doctrine of freedom. You did not even notice that they were opportunists, that the stuff out of which they were made resists the assimilation of the spirit that you have tried to infuse into their hearts! They crucified you. You knew why, but you are, as you were then, stubborn. Your love must be stubborn. Who stood by your side when you carried that cross and bleeding under its weight? Who, among your glorious disciples, was willing to help and share your burden—the burden of freedom and responsibility? All your disciples and friends abandoned you. Even that hypocrite Thomas did not believe in your message. When you joined your father in Heaven, they established The Church in your name but according to their values. They weaved a robe made up of your values.

They wore this robe in public but administered the life of their flock according to their understanding of human nature and destiny. They preach the values of love, but in practice, they preach the values of the Devil: power, pleasure, security, hypocrisy, survival, deception, oppression, fame, and glory. My flock, not yours, behave like sheep. They are expected to be meek, submissive, patient, perseverant, faithful, hardworking, and forgiving. As you can see, the Church places a high value on peace and order. Disorder is one of its worst enemies. You are a disturber of the peace; therefore, you are persona non grata.

"We have been doing so well ever since your death. The Christian community everywhere is a herd of sheep. We feed them beautiful promises and make them behave according to our will in two ways: by threatening them with hell, fire, and damnation, which is intimidating, and by promising them the Kingdom of Heaven, which is desirable and seductive. Heaven and hell are fictions we concocted because they meet the basic urges in human nature, that is, the urge to enjoy pleasure and avoid pain. We know human nature much better than you. We know that they are wolves, and they know that we are a special breed of businesspersons who are hungry for power, but we pretend that we do not see or hear. Survival is our supreme value!

"Yes, we have been doing just fine. Why did you come now? Have you not yet discovered that your doctrine of freedom is impractical and undesirable, that the ideal of humanity, the humanity you envision, is no more than an ideal in your imagination? Oh, no, you are a disturber of the peace. People like you are not allowed to live in our midst. We cannot permit you to return; therefore, you will die tomorrow!"

Just before leaving the prison cell, the silent Jesus, who was speaking profoundly in his silence, moved closer to the ruler of the City of Man and planted a warm kiss on the Inquisitors' lips. No one knew, knows, or will ever know what happened between the two rulers or how they felt, but we know that the ruler of the City of Man threw a glance at Jesus and asked him to leave Seville and never to return to it again. The death sentence was swept with the wind.

Analysis of the Parable

This parable is composed of two metaphors in dialogue with each other, the first is the figure of Jesus, and the second is the figure of the Inquisitor. They form an organic unity; we cannot comprehend the one without the other. I would also add that the relationship that exists between them is dynamical and, moreover, dialectical in nature. It bestows a dramatic quality upon the parable; it makes it alluring and, to borrow a term from Aristotle, brilliant not only because it is informative, as I shall momentarily explain, but also because it is aesthetically pleasing. The aesthetic always appeals to the imagination. This appeal instigates the intellect to examine the deeper riches of the vehicle.

As a metaphor, Jesus, the first figure that appears in the parable, represents the Son of God. He embodies the value of The Good: love or freedom. In contrast, the Grand Inquisitor represents the Devil that embodies the value of Evil as a negation or antithesis of The Good. At the level of metaphor, Jesus exists as an idea or as an image. The act of comprehending or knowing this idea consists of recognizing a set of features that inhere in a human subject, namely, a man who lived in the city of Nazareth as a child, who was known to his people as a prophet, who preached the gospel of love, who cared for the poor, the sick, the disenfranchised, the lonely, and the oppressed, who aroused the dissatisfaction of the establishment, who performed miracles, who was crucified, who viewed himself as the Son of God, who had followers, and who promised those who believed in him eternal life and happiness.

However, the parable of The Grand Inquisitor is not a historical, philosophical, or scientific description. It is a metaphor. The Jesus we meet *in The Brothers Karamazov*, which is a work of fiction, is practically identical to the historical Jesus. He appears 17 centuries later in a social and religious environment that is quite different from the environment in which the historical Jesus lived. Do we or could we meet the real Jesus in Seville or what he represented or stood for? Did Ivan, who narrated the parable, not say that he was going to recite a poem?

Moreover, we know that Jesus is a metaphor because the crowd did not obey him, the Son of God, who was in their midst and performed miracles and because of the kind of conversation he had with the Inquisitor. This conversation was sealed with the most enigmatic, mysterious, baffling, burning kiss one can imagine. Jesus's action was the basis of the metaphor: he was in his action, and he was his action. In both modes of being, when he appeared in Seville and performed two miracles, which spoke more eloquently than the speech of the Inquisitor in the prison cell, he was a living embodiment of the Son of God we find in the Bible.

It is, I think, reasonable to articulate the ontic structure of the metaphor as "Jesus is The Good." In this context, "Jesus" is the ground of the metaphor, and "The Good" is its vehicle. Unlike the Jesus, with whom we are familiar, The Good is a stranger. But then, what is The Good? How can we comprehend this concept? Most people are not familiar with it, and those who are cannot define it, because it has an unexhaustive wealth of meaning. And yet, we see The Good as an image before eyes; we intuit it in this image. However, The Good is infinite; this is why it is suggestive in character. Does it denote all types of goodness, the universal Good, the source of all goodness, or the really good person? As my reflections should indicate or, at least, suggest the connotation of this vehicle is a wealth of meaning. I can even say that the kind of good implied in this vehicle is densely multivalent, in the sense that it signifies a web of multidimensional, interrelated meanings.

First, we may interpret "The Good" metaphysically; as such, the concept would denote the ultimate Good—God, the creator, or the source of the universe. Such a being is infinite in goodness, power, and wisdom. Each one of these concepts—love and freedom—is abundantly rich in its significations or meanings. Second, we may interpret "The Good" epistemologically, in the sense it is the ultimate object of knowledge. We may call this good "substance," The One," God," "First Mover," "will," or "The Absolute." What matters for our purpose in this discourse is whether in philosophy, science, or theology, knowledge of any dimension or aspect of reality necessarily leads to an inquiry into *the ultimate* that underlies the universe. Is the passion of the cosmologist, the metaphysician, or the theologian not a passion for the ultimate that underlies the universe? Was Plato mistaken when he said that the universe was created because its creation was good? Again, did he not suggest that the knowledge of the Good is the noblest kind of knowledge? Third, we may interpret the Good morally in the sense that it is the source and foundation of the moral values that express the essential demands of human nature. A life that is not built on a solid firm foundation will always be vitiated by uncertainty. Can I feel the hope, courage, patience, even the satisfaction I need in everyday living if my life-project and the values on which it stands are not truly and finally justifiable? But how can they be valid if they are not founded in an ultimate that renders them justifiable? Fourth, we may interpret "The Good" as a model of the truly good human being, one who embodies, in the way they think, feel, and act, the finest human qualities. This aspect of meaning was first emphasized by Aristotle in Book One of the *Ethics*. He argued that the moral character of the young develops by (a) experience and (b) imitation, that is, by doing the good and avoiding the bad and by imitating the wise, the sage, or the saintly people. Broadly speaking, we find such people in all, if not most, cultures of the world.

Although very briefly, I mention these four possible interpretations of "The Good" only because each one suggests a possible domain or realm of meaning. Philosophers, theologians, physicists, and artists have been trying to explore, during the past 26,000 years, the inexhaustible wealth of meaning in these and other domains of inquiry. Thus, when I utter in a gathering "Jesus is The Good," this statement will suggest one or more of these domains of meaning. Those who hear this statement do not focus their attention on "Jesus" but on "The Good" because it is new to them. One of the hearers may be a philosopher; accordingly, they may be lured into a mediation on the nature of The Good. However, the hearer may be a curious mind; in this case, they may feel a desire to inquire into the vast realm of The Good. The point that calls for special attention here is that the target in a metaphorical statement is a vehicle of knowledge. The knowledge may be simple or unusually complex, deep, and suggestive of new possible meanings.

Next, the Grand Inquisitor is a metaphor—he represents the Devil. The ontic structure of this metaphor is "The Grand Inquisitor is the Devil." This structure is revealed (a) when the crowd obeyed him but not Jesus, (b) in the conversation he had with Jesus in the prison cell, in which he tried to convince Jesus that the majority of humanity does not want freedom, and (c) in his argument that while Jesus may be in charge of the City of God, he was in charge of the City of Man. Accordingly, in "The Grand Inquisitor is the Devil," "the Grand Inquisitor" is the ground of the metaphor and the Devil is the vehicle. When someone utters this statement, our attention directly moves from the ground to the vehicle because we are familiar with the concept of the Grand Inquisitor but not with the concept of the Devil, though we may think we do. Even a philosopher, or a theologian, cannot comprehend this concept easily or completely because, like the concept of The Good, its connotation is multidimensional and multivalent in character. Yet, the character that embodies this connotation stands before our mind as a human being, not merely as a simple object or idea, but as a world of values and action. (This world is the world of the aesthetic object that emerges in the course of the aesthetic experience. In this world, I intuit what it means for a being to be the Devil and what it means for the Grand Inquisitor to be the Devil. I also intuit what it means to be the Son of God and what it means for Jesus to be the Son of God.)

But the question implied in this metaphor is "What is evil?" We may distinguish two types of evil: human and natural. The first, for example, hate, murder, selfishness, deception, theft, oppression, or injustice, is caused by human beings and the second, for example, earthquakes, volcanos, disease, death, drought, or floods, is caused by nature. Although the Inquisitor embodies human evil, the metaphor necessarily widens the dimension of the ideas suggested by the vehicle. Can you imagine the immensity of the evil of suppressing freedom or love by the establishment of the Church? The primary purpose of the Church is the promotion of freedom, but the Church seems to undermine this purpose. How is this idea depicted in a novel?

The Good arrives in the city of Seville and acts the way Jesus did in Nazareth 700 centuries ago. The Grand Inquisitor apprehends him and condemns him to death. What evil is greater than to trample on the shining presence of The Good or to dim the light of life in the minds, wills, and hearts of a whole population? How can we comprehend the enormity of this evil if we do not probe into its sources? Are the arguments of the Grand Inquisitor justifiable, or is Jesus naive in his endeavor to preach the gospel of freedom? The point of these questions is not to criticize or point a negative finger at the church but to focus on the power of the metaphor as a vehicle of knowledge. Could it be that, in writing this scene, Dostoevsky was trying to say that the church was failing in its mission to preach the gospel of freedom, that it has been reduced to a secular institution, and that it is being governed by a human, not by the divine mind and will? I do not expect answers to these and the earlier questions I raised. Their purpose is to spotlight the structure of the metaphor as a figure of speech and especially the logic of its capacity to communicate philosophical knowledge.

I pointed out earlier that, as metaphors, Jesus and the Grand Inquisitor are joined by a dialectical relation that is made up of thesis and antithesis—good and evil. The medium of this relation is the conversation that took place in the prison cell. Although this conversation was silent and seems to be one-sided, as Jesus did not speak, it was, in fact, quite active, indeed turbulent, not only because Jesus spoke in his silence but also because the enigmatic kiss he pressed on the lips of the Grand Inquisitor sealed the conversation and inspired the Inquisitor to suspend the death sentence. This kiss signaled the formation of a higher metaphorical dimension.

The death sentence symbolized the tyranny of the Inquisitor and his commitment to the values, or rather, disvalues, of the devil. Jesus' kiss symbolized the power of his commitment to the value of freedom. We can view the conversation as a confrontation between good and evil—thesis and antithesis, which is the basis of a type of metaphor on par with analogy, allegory, parable, or fable. We can also view the confrontation as a duel or clash between good and evil, the divine and the earthly. It is obvious that Jesus won the duel for two reasons. First, even though the Grand Inquisitor sentenced Jesus to death, Jesus pressed a kiss of love on his lips. It signified the triumph of the divine over the earthly. Jesus acted exactly the way he did 17 centuries ago. He confirmed the primacy of freedom as the highest ideal of humanity. However, more importantly, he confirmed that he was the true Son of God. Did Jesus not become one with God on the cross? Did he not become one with him again in that kiss? Second, the fire of that kiss transformed the Inquisitor into a momentary believer in the power and supremacy of love in human life. How can the human condemn the divine to death?

REFERENCES AND SUGGESTED BIBLIOGRAPHY

Aristotle. *Poetics and Rhetoric.* (2005) Translated by Eugene Garver, Barnes and Noble.

CHAPTER 6

The Question of Truth in the Philosophical Novel

INTRODUCTION

My relentless critic would now intervene: "Many philosophical novels contain substantial philosophical ideas, views, even arguments, and some critics refer to them as "philosophical," but many of these novels are neither philosophical nor do they belong to a special genre that we can characterize as being philosophical. For a literary novel to be truly philosophical, it should radiate philosophicalness. You have argued that the mere presence of philosophical ideas in a literary novel does not make it philosophical. You have also argued that a literary novel is a world and that this world emerges in the aesthetic experience as an aesthetic object. For example, if a literary novel is romantic, the novel and not merely some of its elements would be romantic. The reader of the novel would experience romanticness as an essential aspect or quality of its world; put differently, its romanticness would shine from the novel the way light shines from the sun so that its romantic aura would permeate every moment of the unfolding aesthetic object.

"First, how can the aesthetic reader feel and know that they are reading a philosophical novel, or does philosophicalness shine through the narrative that they are reading? Again, how can the aesthetic object of a philosophical novel radiate philosophicalness? Can we call a literary novel philosophical if it does not radiate philosophicalness? What makes it radiate philosophicalness? You mentioned this feature in passing earlier, but you did not provide an explanation or a justification of your claim. Such an explanation is urgently needed.

"Second, philosophers aim at true ideas. They advance arguments, explanations, demonstrations and, sometimes, empirical observations or evidence to support their claims; in short, the ideas they propose are tested or verified. They are supposed to attract general assent. Can a philosophical novel be convincing? Can the philosophical novelist argue? As you can see, I would like to know whether the philosophical novelist can do what the philosopher does. But if they cannot, in what sense can their novel be philosophical? For example, can we treat Tolstoy's *The Death of Ivan Ilych*, which portrays the question of the meaning of human life elegantly, absorbingly, strikingly, and profoundly without presenting arguments and explanations as a philosophical novel? Ivan frequently argues philosophically. His arguments may or may not contribute to the literary and philosophical richness and power of the novel, but they are not what makes it philosophical. Suppose it is philosophical, can the insight or knowledge one acquires from reading it be said to be true or convincing? Again, suppose a reader says yes, would 'true' in this literary context be similar to 'true' in a philosophical context? Do not smile if I ask whether metaphors or figures of speech in general can argue or be convincing."

I should begin my discussion with a response to the first question because the answer to the second question presupposes an answer to the first: How does the philosophicalness of the literary novel come to life as a shinning presence in the aesthetic object as a world of meaning? We cannot say whether the knowledge communicated by the philosophical novel is convincing or true, at least to a reasonable extent, unless we know the mode of existence of philosophicalness.

Mode of Existence of Philosophicalness

I have argued in the first two chapters that the philosophical novel is composed of three strata: the text the novelist creates, the aesthetic qualities that inhere in the text as a significant form, and the aesthetic object that emerges in the aesthetic experience. The first stratum comprises a narrative, or story, the second comprises the unity of the aesthetic qualities that inhere in the narrative as a significant form, and the third comprises the structure of the aesthetic object that comes to life in the aesthetic experience as a world of meaning. The first and second strata exist for the sake of the third stratum.

6 THE QUESTION OF TRUTH IN THE PHILOSOPHICAL NOVEL   121

I have also argued that the theme of the literary novel exists as a potentiality in the significant form that unfolds with the unfolding of the aesthetic object. The theme I comprehend when I read the literary novel as a story is different from the theme I comprehend when I read it as a literary work of art. For example, when I read Dostoevsky's *The Idiot*, I discover that its themes revolve around a Russian prince who was in a sanatorium in Switzerland on his way to his hometown in Russia. Soon after he carves a niche for himself in the local community, he bungles every social relation he establishes, exposes himself to ridicule, and loses his money foolishly. In short, everyone in his social circle treats him as an idiot. He comes from a sanatorium, after all! Even the woman who falls in love with him abandons him. He feels naked. He cannot stay anymore in Russia. He decides to return to the sanatorium in Switzerland.

Anyone who reads this literary novel as a story would, I think, discover the same theme because, as a story, it is given as a ready-made reality, that is, as a historical account of an adventure. However, an aesthetic reading of the way Prince Myshkin behaves would reveal that he is a Jesus figure. He is always tolerant, forgiving, loving, modest, generous, respectful, peaceful, honest, and courageous. In short, he embodies the values of Jesus in the way he speaks and acts. Yet, his society taunts him and almost everyone abuses him. He decides to return to the sanatorium. Could it be that the sanatorium is the proper place for truly decent, genuine human beings, or could it be that the sanatorium is the right place for good people? How else can they be protected against the harm inflicted by the ignorant, selfish, cunning, and sanctimonious society? How can a lamb survive in a society of wolves?

I have already discussed the metaphorical dimension of *The Idiot*. Though briefly, I mention it only to expand the realm of analysis of the critic's question: How does philosophicalness radiate from the novel so that the novel as a whole declares its philosophicalness when one reads it aesthetically? The proposition I shall now elucidate is that in order for the novel to declare its philosophical identity, every scene, character, conversation, action, description, or incident should not only be *organically* related to the theme of the novel but also reflect the meaning implicit in it.

Let us take another look at the Grand Inquisitor scene. Jesus' visit to the city of Seville was the visit of a shepherd to his flock or the visit of a priest to his churchgoers. It was not the grand visit promised by the historical Jesus 17 centuries ago. Nevertheless, the God-fearing citizens of the city of Seville recognized him: he was the real Jesus, the same Jesus they read about in the Bible, the same Jesus who was crucified, the same Jesus they worshipped every Sunday, and the same Jesus who would grant eternal life and happiness! The Grand Inquisitor, who was watching him and every action he performed and how he performed them, also recognized him. He was displeased by what he saw, and thus, he sentenced Jesus to death on the following day.

However, the Grand Inquisitor decided to visit Jesus in his prison cell that night. The two characters had a one-sided conversation in which the Inquisitor spoke and Jesus remained silent. At the end of the conversation, Jesus pressed a warm kiss on the Inquisitor's lips. Stunned, baffled, and intrigued by that kiss, the Inquisitor suspended the death sentence and asked him to leave with the proviso that Jesus would not return to Seville.

Please reflect on this scene the way Dostoevsky presented it in *The Brothers Karamazov*. How can the real theme of this scene be an encounter or a duel between God and the Devil, freedom and oppression, or the forces of good and evil? How does the reader first glean and gradually know that the majority of human beings do not want freedom and the burden of responsibility it entails? How can the church that is supposed to be the true guardian and promoter of the ideals of Jesus be transformed into a secular institution that does not give a hoot about those ideals but simply acts on the dictum that human beings can "live by bread alone"? How can faith in the Son of God be a hollow faith?

Again, how can the duel between the Inquisitor and Jesus or between Good and Evil, which proceeds slowly from the moment Jesus appears on the steps of Cathedral of Seville to the moment he leaves the prison come to life as an aesthetic object when one reads this story, of course, as an integral part of the whole novel? How can this object, which exists potentially in the story as a significant form, emerge in the aesthetic experience? I think that the answer to this question lies in the secret of the creative vision of the novelist—in *the way he formed the plot* of the story. Well, what about this way *enables* it to be a potentiality for the real theme of the encounter between Jesus and the Grand Inquisitor?

This way originates from the author's creative vision that gives rise to the details of the story. This vision has its own way of seeing a certain content of meaning and the form in which it can be expressed or communicated adequately. We cannot give a logical explanation to how it—the vision—chooses its form; on the contrary, it is the source of its own logic—the logic of how to articulate the content of meaning and communicate it truthfully, clearly, and dramatically. This logic is the source of the unity of the story; it is what enables every element to cohere with the other elements. It is also what enabled the novelist to infuse the form he chose with the real theme of the novel. For example, is the crowd's obedience to the Inquisitor and the renunciation of their loyalty to the Son of God not logically consistent with the Inquisitor's thesis that he is the devil and that the way of the Church is his way? Again, is this renunciation not consistent with the ideas and actions of the Inquisitor in the prison cell? Moreover, does the scene in which the crowd obeys the Inquisitor not whisper in the ear of the reader that they do not want freedom and that they had chosen the way of the Inquisitor? How can you bite the hand that feeds you? Had the hand of Jesus fed them bread? Would they have abandoned him had he fed them bread? No, that hand sought to give them freedom. However, which should come first—bread or freedom?

The capacity of each element of the Grand Inquisitor scene to radiate philosophicalness originates from the same creative vision that gave rise to them and by virtue of which they are organically unified. However, how can the novelist succeed in creating this kind of unity? The medium and means of its creation is the metaphor. As I explained in the preceding chapter, the ontic structure of the metaphor consists of a ground and a vehicle. The ground functions as a subject, and the vehicle as a predicate. The subject does not communicate new ideas because it is assumed to be familiar, but the predicate does because it is new and it is a *possibility* of knowing something new.

The vehicle is cognitive by virtue of its qualitative nature. The qualities that make up its being are cognitive in two ways: They are transformed into meaning in the aesthetic experience and their formal organization is *suggestive* of new meanings. For example, as a metaphorical figure, Jesus stands for The Good. How can he be such if he were not the *Logos*, that is, the Son of God? However, if he is the Son of God, if he is infinite in his being, it would follow that the extent and possibilities of this Good are infinite. Is it an accident that for the majority of Christian theologians, the Word of God is the source and basis of universal wisdom? Do Christians not attribute everything good in the word to God? How many a theologian, beginning with Augustine, argued that God is not responsible for the existence of evil in the world? How can God create something evil? Besides, regardless of whether God is the source of the Good, is the realm of The Good as a value not an inexhaustible possibility for expansion and realization?

It would now be appropriate to say that the organic unity of the various elements of the philosophical novel and the fact that this unity originates from the creative vision that gives rise to it is what enables it to declare its philosophicalness. Accordingly, and in direct response to the critic's question, how does philosophicalness radiate from the novel as a whole? I can say that it does so by the power of the aesthetic object that inheres in it. This object, which makes up the structure of the significant form and is the foundation of its literary dimension, is immanent in every detail of the novel. It begins to radiate when we begin reading it aesthetically, that is, when we assume an aesthetic attitude in the process of reading it. For example, how can I continue to read the Grand Inquisitor scene as an ordinary story after discovering that the crowd who witnessed the miracles and were convinced that the Jesus who performed them was the Son of God but nonetheless was not really loyal to him but to the Inquisitor? How can I treat this scene merely as a story after grasping the significance of the enigmatic, magical kiss at the conclusion of that conversation? I would not be mistaken if I characterize this kiss as an *aesthetic explosion*, one that spoke more than the long lecture of the Inquisitor, one that transformed him into a temporary, perhaps a permanent, believer? How can you refrain or stop yourself from feeling guilty after you know that you pronounced a death sentence on the true Son of God? How can I read *The Idiot* as a mere story after I discover that in everything Mishkin did or said, he exemplified the values and ideals of Jesus? Do I not concomitantly, with this discovery, discover that all the people he interacted with were selfish, opportunistic, cunning, and deceptive? Does this twofold discovery not enable me to see the prince as a spiritual prince and not only as a social prince? Is his social status as a prince, not as a metaphor for being a spiritual prince? Such discoveries mark the gradual emergence of the poem as an aesthetic object that opens up a world within the larger world of *The Brothers Karamazov*.

Domain and Validity of Knowledge in the Philosophical Novel

One of the critic's main questions is, first, whether the philosophical novel can communicate all types of philosophical questions, ideas, or problems; if it does, to what extent can the knowledge it communicates be as certain or reliable as the knowledge the philosopher tries to communicate?

Second, one of the central aims of the philosopher is to articulate their understanding or insight of a dimension of value as a general or universal proposition, one that entails general assent. The critic would raise this question because it would be difficult to view the knowledge communicated by the philosophical novel as serious if it does not communicate reasonably valid knowledge or if the knowledge it communicates is simply subjective or idiosyncratic. The quest for validity in philosophy is central; this is why the philosopher relies on critical analysis, argument, demonstration, and observations in theorizing on any aspect of meaning. However, if the philosophical novelist does not analyze, argue, or demonstrate, I may be asked, should one take the knowledge they communicate seriously? Would a fair-minded person read such a novel in the first place? I shall discuss the first question in this section and devote my attention to the second question in the following section. The proposition I shall clarify and defend is that the philosophical novelist can communicate the type of knowledge the philosopher seeks to communicate and that is neither more nor less certain or valid than the knowledge they seek to communicate.

First, Scope of Knowledge in the Philosophical Novel

An answer to the question of the domain of knowledge in the philosophical novel should, I think, begin with an explanation of the object, type of reality, or medium of reflection in philosophy and the philosophical novel. As I discussed earlier, the realm of reflection in the empirical sciences is constituted by the facts that make up the order of nature, while the realm of reflection in art and philosophy is the *meaning of these facts*. The realm of meaning is the realm of values. Accordingly, the question we need to analyze is whether the philosophical novelist can reflect on some or all types of values and whether they can communicate their insight or understanding of any value question in a literary or artistic symbolic form. My immediate answer to this question is yes. Why?

Regardless of its type and by its very essence, value, as such, is an ideal, and as an ideal, it is a general idea, and as an idea, it is a schema or plan of action. However, ideas, and, consequently, all values do not exist as parts of the furniture of the realm of nature. We do not encounter the ideas of justice, truth, existence, tree, or philosophy anywhere in the garden, the mountain, the plain, the sea, or the marketplace. They exist in the human mind and nowhere else, and they do not exist there as any kind of definable metaphysical, psychological, or physical substances that can be defined the way we define the natural objects around or the mental events in our psyche. Values exist as potentialities for realization in a certain way or form in a concrete situation. For example, the value of justice can be realized in a certain way in a concrete individual or social situation. The way or forms of its realization varies from one situation to another.

Broadly speaking, "potentiality" is a possible type of concrete existence, one that does not yet exist but may exist, that is, its existence is a viable possibility. However, it cannot step into reality from the realm of nothing. *Qua* potentiality, it must exist somewhere and in some way. It exists as an idea in a particular mind. This idea does not fall from the ceiling of the mind, and it does not appear in it accidentally or by the strike of some magical wand. Its birthplace is an intellectual vision, one that comes into being as a result of intense reflection on a logical web of concepts, a practical problem, or a dimension of reality. The capacity of the idea to be a potentiality is derived from the fact that the activity of reflection is, first, based on a meaningful content of thought and, second, logically possible. Its mode of existence is not the mode of existence of material or psychological objects, as I have just indicated, but that of intellectual vision. I here assume that the mind is not reducible to either physical or psychological categories. However, if it is not reducible, and if it exists, what kind of existence is it? This mode of existence is, I submit, pure experience. The *ontic locus* of this type of experience is reflection, and the ontic locus of reflection is the brain. The "I" that undergoes an imaginative or intellectual experience, regardless of the kind of object on which it reflects, rises to a mode of being that transcends the material or the psychological as such. For example, in the heat of any profound experience, we are not usually conscious of anything material or psychological, and we are not conscious that the experience we are having is either psychological or physical. I may characterize it as "spiritual" for lack of a better term. That which is ideal or spiritual is emergent; it comes into being in the womb of reflection. There is no reason for me to propose a theory of mind, for such a proposal is beyond the scope of this discourse. Suffice it to say that, no matter its kind, ideas do not exist as entities in a drawer of the mind or on one of its shelves, for the mind is not a kind of box or shelter of ideas. All ideas exist when an activity of reflection creates an occasion for their emergence from the womb of possibility in the heat of a creative act or for their recollection from the store of memory. This is the main reason why, whether recalled or created, an idea exists as a potentiality for a possible way of thinking, and it exists as a possibility because its content is not yet conceived or thought. It exists, as I said a moment ago, as a potentiality for being a particular idea. For example, I have an idea of a "chair" in my mind. In itself, it lacks a particular content or definable essence. It contains an outline for a possible particular idea. However, it is a potentiality for being a countless formal realization that can be subsumed under the general idea of "chair." Human beings have been conceiving and creating different types of chairs since the dawn of human civilization. This only shows that the general idea of a chair is no more than a schema for a possible creation or conception. However, what is the mode of existence of the general idea of a chair that I can recall from the sphere of my memory? Its mode of existence is that of the mind that, I may venture to propose, emerges into being the moment the human being becomes conscious of themself and their environment.

Let us now ask: What does "value" signify? How do we define this term? The only definition we can provide is a *general* definition, primarily because it exists as a potentiality, not as a concrete psychological or physical object, one that has identifiable features. Accordingly, we can say that "value" signifies "importance," and "importance" signifies that which matters in human life, that which we prize, or that which is worthwhile. However, what is the signification of the "that" in the preceding sentence? It signifies objects, relations, qualities, or the types of experiences that meet the essential needs or demands of human nature. We may classify these needs or demands into three basic categories: the true, the good, and the beautiful. Each one of these categories signifies a basic value, and each value has, in turn, a large number of derivative values. We seek these values because their realization in our individual lives is the basis and source of happiness; put differently, their realization makes our lives meaningful.

As bodies, we live in the realm of nature, but as human beings, we live in the realm of values. An investigative look at the history of human civilization will readily show that the realm of values is constantly growing and expanding. In itself, it is indeterminate. Whether it is the good, the true, the beautiful, or any of their derivatives, they are values because they are modes of importance. The important, as such, is an infinite sea of potentiality that can be concretized in infinite ways. This sea is, to borrow a term from Whitehead, an inexhaustible wealth of potentiality. It is the ultimate field of inquiry of the philosopher and the artist. The first reflects on the multitude of its possibilities and expresses their intuition of any one of its dimensions or any aspect of these dimensions and articulates it conceptually. The painter reflects on a dimension or an aspect and articulates their intuition of it pictorially; similarly, the musician articulates their intuition acoustically, the dancer articulates their intuition dynamically, and the philosophical novelist articulates their intuition depictively. No one creator, regardless of the means of their expression has, as I indicated earlier, a monopoly on any dimension of meaning as an inexhaustible wealth of potentiality, primarily because it is given as an objective fact, and it is such a fact because the meaning the philosopher or the artist seeks is the meaning of these facts. This claim is based on the assumption that value, or meaning, is amenable to articulation in any possible symbolic form. This is why we can translate the meaning expressed in one kind of artwork into other kinds of artworks, and this is why we can translate the meaning of a philosophical work into different types of artworks. Do we not encounter values such as justice, grace, joy, love, beauty, or grandeur in both philosophical and artistic works? Do art teachers not explain the kind of values expressed in certain artworks conceptually, and do art critics not do the same when they evaluate artworks aesthetically? I should hasten to add that not only values but also their opposites, viz., disvalues, are common themes in art and philosophy.

In view of what I said so far, it would be reasonable to say that any area of value discussed or which may be discussed by the philosopher can, in principle, be communicated by the philosophical novelist. If this claim is granted, it should follow that any value discussed by the philosopher is an appropriate subject of expression by the artist in general and the philosophical novelist in particular. We should remember that creative expression in art and philosophy is an activity in which the creator reflects on the sea of meaning *qua* potentiality and articulates their intuition of a dimension of this sea in a particular symbolic form. The nature of this activity is implied by the word "to express"—"ex" and "premere" together mean "to force out" as "ex" means "out" and "premere" means "to press." The activity of intuition is one in which the philosopher or the artist "presses out" or gives a particular form to a dimension of meaning that exists as a potentiality.

What matters in human life is not derived from a pre-existing law, principle, and divine or political decree but originates from the bosom of the human condition. Whether it is an aesthetic, moral, political, or social, value judgment or expression is an existential response to a human need felt in a concrete, lived moment or situation. The concept of value implies that we should meet the essential demands or needs of human nature, but how we meet these needs or demands arises from the concrete situations of our lives.

Second, Question of Certainty in the Philosophical Novel

Proposition is the symbolic form in which the philosopher communicates their knowledge; *depiction*, or pictorial image, is the symbolic form in which the philosophical novelist communicates their knowledge. The first is the outcome of a process of logical reasoning; the second is the outcome of direct intuition. However, the activities of logical reasoning and artistic intuition are preceded by what I called in the first chapter of this book *pre-reflective or pre-symbolic* meditation on a certain dimension or aspect of value. The philosopher communicates their knowledge by means of a conceptual framework and the artist by means of a figure of speech. The philosopher *argues* logically; the philosophical novelist *presents* the content of their intuition in a symbolic form. The philosophical reader comprehends the philosophical truth by thinking it, and the literary reader comprehends it by direct intuition, primarily because it is a *luminous presence*.

One of the main aims of the philosopher is to provide truthful or valid knowledge. The means of establishing truth or validity is argument, demonstration, and observation. Tested knowledge is expected to be certain, that is, clear, capable of inter-subjective assent, and convincing. This feature is critically important because people would not take philosophical knowledge or any other type of knowledge seriously if it is not reliable, and it cannot be reliable if it is not certain or if it does not work. However, the philosophical novelist presents their knowledge, and this knowledge is not tested. It is acquired in intuition, and it is acquired through communication. However, it seems difficult to determine whether it is true, and if it is true, how its truth is established. The question that concerns my critic is whether the kind of knowledge the philosophical novelist presents is or can be certain. If it is or can be certain, how do we know? Therefore, the following remark is in order.

Although the philosopher establishes the truth of their knowledge by the method of logical reasoning, demonstration, and observation, the aspect of the truth or falsity of their knowledge depends on the extent to which their reflection on, or comprehension of, the given datum of meaning is or is not complete or adequate. The activity of reasoning or demonstration is a later undertaking. Its purpose is to establish the truth or adequacy of this comprehension. Indeed, the adequacy of this comprehension is, I think, the ultimate test of the truth or falsity of philosophical knowledge. Do we not support or refute a philosophical theory or proposition on the basis of the adequate or inadequate comprehension of the content of meaning we seek to communicate symbolically? Do we not establish the validity of a theory or proposition by showing that the theory or proposition fails to explain this or that aspect of the fact they are said to explain, that is, by trying to show that the comprehension of the primary intuition that give rise to the theory or proposition is inadequate? But then, how do we know whether the knowledge communicated by the philosopher is more or less adequate than that of the philosophical novelist? The first tries to prove the validity of their knowledge but the second simply presents it and the reader can "take it or leave it."

Certainty had been a central aim in philosophy until the end of the twentieth century; it had also been a thorny and controversial question. I cannot even begin to discuss it, much less participate in the controversy or move through its thorns without a lengthy debate. Nevertheless, it is important to remark that absolute certainty in philosophy as well as in science is not possible not only because human nature and physical reality are constantly changing but also because the means of knowing nature and human nature are constantly progressing quantitatively and qualitatively. Instead of aiming to determine absolute certainties, philosophers, scientists, and even artists aim at a kind of knowledge that works or that produces useful or satisfactory results. I tend to think that the ultimate test for the adequacy of any type of knowledge is not whether it conforms to an established criterion, standard, or principle but the extent to which it enables us to grow as human beings at the individual and social levels, expand our knowledge of physical reality, and unlock the secret of the creative powers of the human mind.

We may choose this aim in evaluating the truth and validity of philosophical knowledge, but even if we do, we remain confronted with the challenge of the critic: Can the knowledge communicated by the philosophical novelist be as truthful, adequate, or workable as the knowledge communicated by the philosopher? My answer to this question is a resounding yes. *First,* the interactions and collaboration between the world of philosophy and that of literature have been active and productive ever since the rise of Western civilization in ancient Greece. Did the ancient philosophers, especially Plato, not learn from and teach the poets, novelists, and dramatists of that period? This kind of interaction has remained active to the present day. Many of the great poets, such as Shelley, Wordsworth, Whitman, and Eliot, and many of the great novelists, such as Proust, Melville, Dostoevsky, and Mann, not to mention existentialist novelists, such as Sartre, G. Marcel, or Camus, are vivid examples of the cooperation between the philosophical and literary minds. Even a cursory examination of the serious novels in the past 300 years will assuredly show that they deal with some of the basic questions, problems, and concerns of human life. Is it an accident that a novelist such as Sir Walter Scott would remark that a novel that does not have a moral should not be written or taken seriously or for the English philosopher John Locke to say that a book that does not advance our knowledge should not be written or read?

Second, and apart from the prevalence of philosophical themes in literature, especially in the novel, it is reasonable to state that, in principle, the kind of knowledge the philosophical novelist communicates can be as profound, truthful, and instructive as the knowledge communicated by the philosopher, if not more. Let me illustrate the reasonableness of this claim by analysis of the theme of a novel we have already visited—the question of the meaning of human life in Tolstoy's *The Death of Ivan Ilych*.

The focus of this novel is on the value of authenticity. We should be familiar with the plot of this novel because I have already discussed its main theme. We can now examine how the question of the meaning of human life is *presented through the mode of depiction* and especially how Tolstoy discloses the significance and truth of authenticity as a supreme human value. It is important to point at the outset that the main character, Ivan, is a metaphor that represents the inauthentic human being and whose life represents the inauthentic human life. We can also call him Mr. Inauthentic Man. I propose this characterization because he embodies in the way he thinks, feels, and lives the essential features that make a human being inauthentic.

The idea of inauthenticity is the opposite of the idea of authenticity. Now, what makes a person authentic? Or, what are the essential qualities—psychological, moral, social, intellectual, aesthetic, religious—that make a person authentic? Broadly speaking, such a person is, first, honest, generous, courageous, trustworthy, truthful, and modest—in short, moral, socially, and professionally upright. Second, they are a human individual. By "individual," I here mean one who acts from within, from their heart, mind, and will, not from the heart, mind, and will of others, regardless of whether the "others" is society, friends, the state, tradition, or merely their ideology. Third, they are a growing, progressive human being, in the sense that they meet their intellectual, affective, aesthetic, and political needs; put differently, they respect and observe the laws that govern their nature as a human being. Hypocrisy, deception, laziness, and selfishness are some of their enemies. They derive their happiness from their achievements as an individual, not as a gift or favor they receive from others. If I am to characterize them metaphorically, I can say that the authentic person is the shepherd of their life. In contradistinction to this characterization, the inauthentic person is a sheep in a herd of sheep governed by a shepherd who may be good or evil. The shepherd is the reason for their existence and identity.

Now, suppose we ask a philosopher to give us an account of the identity of the authentic human being—what kind of account would we receive from them? Generally speaking, the kind of account we may receive would be systematic, propositional, reasoned, and conceptually coherent. But then, let us also ask them to give us an account of how they would face their death when they reach the last station of their life, that is, how they would make a transition from the realm of being into the realm of eternal oblivion. I think the account they would give can be distilled into one word: stoically!

When I give this possible answer, I mean that the authentic person would think, feel, and act rationally: knowingly, calmly, contentedly, modestly, and willingly; they would not fret or complain, although they would rationally feel sad because they would be missing the joy of life, which would be temporary. Have they not recognized that change is king, that nothing is permanent, that all human beings die or will sooner or later die, and that they are a human being, and therefore, they will die? Are they the author of the laws that govern the natural process? They can govern their ideas, emotions, and will, but can they influence the laws of nature? Can they rebel against them?

Suppose we ask this philosopher to give us a characterization of how the inauthentic person would think, feel, and act when they reach the last station of their life and when they recognize that their death is around the corner—what would their account be like? I think their answer can be distilled into one word: frantically!

When I say frantically, I mean, first, they would be confused because they had not thought about the facticity of transience or their individual transience. Their realization that they had reached the very end would be a devastating surprise to them. At the existential level, they had lived their life as if they would not die, as if death was not a part of their life, or at least that death would not touch them. They had been growing old, yes, but they dismissed this idea from their consciousness not only because they were able to adjust to this ongoing process of aging but also because "death" happens to others but not to them and because they could not imagine their own death or their non-existence. Second, they would feel angry primarily because they had lived on the quiet assumption that life, and especially their life, was a right. Neither death nor any other kind of power could deprive them of this right. However, death has been waiting for them for a long time, and now, it is around the corner. They feel cornered. What kind of emotions, feelings, and ideas would visit a person who finds himself stuck in the last or only "corner" of their life? Third, in that corner, the inauthentic person would feel guilty because they cannot live anymore in the present of the future and because they cannot fantasize about this or that kind of life; thus, they reflect on their past life. However, alas, what kind of life do they reflect on? A sham life, a life of self-deception, a life they cannot claim as their own because it did not arise from their mind, heart, and will but from the mind, heart, and will of the shepherd that tended their life and the life of their herd—from the mind, heart, and will of the almighty "they." How would you feel, dear reader, if just before you discover that your life had been a sham and that you wasted the most precious gift you received when you entered the world of the living? Would you not feel guilty? By "guilt" in this context, I do not mean moral, social, or psychological guilt. No, I mean ontological guilt, the kind that originates from the core of your being, the kind you feel when you are tried before a jury of your conscience for the nastiest, most catastrophic crime you could commit, viz., the crime of self-abnegation.

Although briefly and to some extent sketchily presented, the primary purpose of discussing the concept of authenticity and its contrary is simply to raise the question of the meaning of human life: What makes the life of a human being worth living? Philosophers, artists, and theologians would, I think, agree that leading an authentic life is the source of happiness: authenticity is the defining feature of the meaningful way of life. I here assume, as I indicated a moment ago, that the authentic person is true to themselves when they meet the demands of their daily life and when they continue to grow as a human individual.

Now, let us shift our attention to the central question of *The Death of Ivan Ilych*, namely, the question of the meaning of human life. I would not be too amiss if I propose that Tolstoy's view of the meaning of human life accords with the view of the majority of philosophers, if not all of them.

The concordance between these two types of views is, of course, general. It is possible for one to be truer, deeper, clearer, or more convincing than the other. However, what is important for my discussion is that the conceptual content of meaning of the philosopher's account can, in principle, be communicated depictively, that is, without the use of logical or conceptual analysis and certainly without appealing to any type of test or verification. As I shall momentarily emphasize, the literary image can be as cognitive and communicative as the logical argument and conceptual analysis of the philosopher. I would not be surprised if a philosophical novelist argues that the philosophical novel can be more cognitive, more powerful, more convincing than theories or conceptions of the philosopher. Be that as it may, and in deference to my critic, who is anxious to know how a philosophical novel can communicate philosophical knowledge, it is important to explain how Tolstoy communicates his understanding of the meaning of human life depictively.

The *Death of Ivan Ilych* is, to begin, a narrative; it is not a set of propositions that logically leads to a conclusion or that concludes with a conception of the meaning of human life. An aesthetic reading of this novel would, I think, show that Ivan is an embodiment of the inauthentic person. His inauthenticity reveals itself in two ways: in the way he lived prior to his sickness and in the way he thought, felt, and acted after he knew that the life he had led was a sham.

First, Ivan was a highly successful professional. He was able to climb the social ladder to its acme. He was able to assume one of the highest positions in the legal institution. Successful and respectable people sought his friendship, and many young women were delighted at the prospect of marrying him. In fact, his circle of friends was socially and professionally distinguished, and he married a young woman generally recognized for her beauty and high social rank. Ivan was in a position of envy. He was admired and feared mainly because he was powerful and effective in his work.

However, Ivan was a conformist. He was not the author of his ideas and way of living. His ideas did not originate from his mind, his feelings did not originate from his heart, and his actions did not originate from his will. On the contrary, his mind, heart, and will were extensions of the *social* mind, heart, and will. If I am to express this point succinctly, I can say that, at the human level, he was a hollow person. The tragic side of his character is that he did not know that he was a hollow person; in other words, he did not know that the mind, heart, and will that pulsated in his being were fictions concocted by the indefinable "they." Moreover, he did not know that the friends he had were fair-weather friends. Worse still, he did not know that the happiness he thought he was enjoying was false.

Second, the moment Ivan reached the last step of his ascent to the highest level of his professional advancement, he had a freaky accident that marked the beginning of a long, tortuous, calamitous, hideous, and irreversible descent into the land of death. At the beginning of this descent, he thought that his sickness was temporary, that he would assume his new position soon, and that he would reap the happiness of his great achievements. However, in contrast to his hope, his sickness was more serious than he had thought. When this idea loomed in the sky of his consciousness, when he realized that it was a fact that no one, not even the doctor, could change, when he stared into the dark tunnel of his existence through which was gliding into the land of eternal oblivion, he underwent a radical change of consciousness in which he acquired new eyes and new capacities of thinking, feeling, and willing. This change was revolutionary because, for the first time, he began to think, feel, and will from his inner, real self.

However, although he was transformed into a new being, still, he was unable to accept the fact that the tunnel into which he was sliding was real. He did not want to die! He did not deserve to die! He struggled with this brutal fact for several days; he discussed it with his doctor and begged him to save him from that descent, as if the doctor was the author of his life or of the laws of nature. He reasoned logically against it with the power of his logical mind only to see the face of death staring him in the eyes. Mockingly, those eyes spoke, "It is time, Ivan! Are you ready?"

Oh, how human beings become masters of rationalization when they are under psychological and social pressure and especially when their existence is threatened! Life is dear, but suddenly Ivan realized that his life, the new life he had just discovered was dearer, infinitely dearer than all the glory of the social world he was striving to enjoy. He also realized that, in the midst of all the agony he was suffering, the life he had led was a big sham. How would you feel, dear reader, if you discover, just before you are leaving this world that you have blundered your way into the world of death before you even began to live? Can you escape the piercing claws of guilt? Can you ignore the pain that gushes out of their ruthless bites? Can you sit still anymore? Can you determine with any measure of certainty where you are but within the flames of torment and agony that seem to gnaw your consciousness without regard to your feelings or desires?

Torment, suffering, agony? No, these words cannot capture the heat of the volcano of misery Ivan was experiencing during the last three days of his "existence." I refrained from using the word "life" because he was not living, because he had never lived, because he had simply existed. In fact, *he was living the death of his life and the life of his death*! The realization just before you die that your life has been a sham oozes the nastiest odor you can inhale through your psychological nostrils.

An irony intensified the agony Ivan was experiencing during that torment. One of his peasants, Gerasim, who was nursing him, was a shining star of life, innocence, modesty, realism, understanding, and patience. He served his master studiously, honestly, respectfully, calmly, and effectively without complaining and without expressing any feeling of dissatisfaction at the repulsive sight of his master. It is appropriate to say that this peasant was an embodiment of the authentic human being. I have a hunch that Ivan realized this fact. With a stroke of genius, Tolstoy created a vivid contrast between the authentic and inauthentic person.

Please, dear reader, imagine that the bartender of your life has prepared for you a cocktail made of the nastiest bout of guilt, agony, and frenzy; yes, imagine this drink flowing into your belly, and imagine that it settles in every fiber of your being for several days—how would you feel? I am confident that you would feel that the earth under your feet is quaking, that you are swirling in a crushing whirlwind, and that the dim light which is enfolding you refuses to reach your eyes! The only thing you can do when the tormenting effect of this drink overcomes your mind, heart, and will is scream—not this or that scream but the scream that originates from the universal scream, the scream that flows from the belly of the forces of evil in this universe. And this is exactly what Ivan did during the last three days of his life. His existence was one with this scream. It was so powerful and devastating that Gerasim, who was a pure light of goodness and fortitude, stood amid the reverberations of that scream with total bafflement. Of course, Ivan's wife and his children rushed into his room more than once not to solace him or show their love for him, and certainly not to pity him, but to make sure that his condition would not obstruct the planning of his daughter's wedding that was supposed to take place on the following Sunday. He watched the spectacle they created, and he understood its meaning. At that moment a stream of warm light, of love, surged from the depth of his heart. He felt sorry for them, and he pitied them. He wanted to say that he loved them and that he forgave them, but he could not because his first foot was already in the land of eternal oblivion.

In *The Death of Ivan Ilych*, Tolstoy does not analyze the question of the meaning of human life, and he does not try to prove that his understanding of this question is true. He simply wrote a literary novel. However, as I tried to show in the preceding paragraphs, he created a living image, a *luminous literary presence* of the question of the meaning of human life. This question is written in the narrative of the life and death of Ivan Ilych. One reads it in the aesthetic object as it unfolds in the process of reading the novel. Tolstoy created a living image of a man who, in his life and death, discloses the nature of this question. The image Tolstoy created speaks not by means of concepts and arguments but pictorially by enabling us to see what it is like to live as a human being and how to die as a human being. The image he created enables the reader to penetrate the stratum of concepts, even of images, and comprehend in it the value of human life. The medium in which this intuition is possible is the spectacle of life and death he created in this novel. Having read this novel, can the reader anymore ignore the facticity of death? Can they ignore that they should design their life-project on the understanding that their life is short? Can they design this project without an understanding of the essential needs or demands of human nature in general and the needs or demands of their life as an individual in particular?

How can you enable the image to speak if you are not an ontological magician, that is, if you cannot infuse the image with the fire of human life, if you cannot form it with a feeling of love, if you cannot endow it with the power of speech, and if you cannot give it a spirit the way the goddess Care infused spirt in the clay out of which human beings were created?

Tolstoy did not begin his novel with an account of Ivan's life; he began it with the scene of his death—of how his family and friends talked about everything meaningless under the sky but the meaning of death or the meaning of sham life. Some were happy that he had died, and some were anxious to get him buried as soon as possible. Did the sight of the dead Ivan provoke the question of the meaning of death in human life? No. The spirit of the first chapter of the novel, of the scent of death, hovers ominously over every description and incident of the novel and reaches a resounding climax in that devastating scream.

Can the literary image speak more or less adequately than the philosophical concept? It is difficult to give a satisfactory answer to this question mainly because some philosophical conceptions speak more lucidly and convincingly than literary images, and some literary images speak more lucidly and convincingly than philosophical conceptions. For example, Tolstoy's *The Death of Ivan Ilych* has, to my mind, depicted the question of the meaning of human life more lucidly and more adequately than any philosophical account of this question. Has this novel not influenced a large number of philosophers and, in some cases, revolutionized their conceptions of the question of the meaning of human life? Has this novel ceased to leave a profound and, in some cases, transformative impact on anyone who reads this novel aesthetically? Again, is it an accident that some of the greatest literary novels are philosophical?

References and Suggested Bibliography

Alphen, Ernst van. (2005) *Art in Mind*. *Chicago:* University of Chicago Press.
Altman, R. (2008). *A Theory of Narrative*. New York: Columbia University Press.
Aristotle. *Poetics and Rhetoric*. (2005) Translated by Eugene Garver, Barnes and Noble.
Bailey, John (1975). *Tolstoy and the Novel*. London: Macmillan.
Beardsley, Monroe (1981). Aesthetics. Indianapolis: Hackett Publishing.
Bell, Clive (1958). *Art*. New York: Capricorn Books.
Berger, Karol. (2002) *A Theory of Art*. Oxford: Oxford University Press.
Berger, John. (1990). *Ways of Seeing*. New York: Penguin.
Berling, Alexis (2016) *Essential Literary Genres*. Mankato, MN: Abdo Publishing.
Bersani, Leo (1965). *Marcel Proust: The Functions of Art and Life*. New York: Macmillan.
Bessone, Frederica. (2017) *The Literary Genres of the Flavian Age*. Berlin: De Gruyter.
Buck, Gertrude. (1899). *The Metaphor: A Study in the Psychology of Rhetoric*. The Inland Press.
Bishop, Tom. (2021). *Literature Is a Voyage of Discovery*. Chicago: University of Chicago Press.
Budd, Malcom. (2012) *Aesthetic Essays*. Oxford: Oxford University Press.
Cassirer, Ernst. (1962). An Esay on Man. New Haven: Yale University Press.
Dadejik, Ondrei. (2021) *Process and Aesthetics*. Chicago: University of Chicago Press.
Danto, A. C. (1985). *Narrative and Knowledge*. New York: Columbia University Press.

Descombes, Vincent (1992). *Proust: Philosophy of the Novel.* Translated by Catherine C. Beardsley. Stanford: Stanford University Press.
Derrida, Jacque (1987). *The Truth of Painting.* Chicago: University of Chicago Press.
Dewey, John (1958). *Art as Experience.* New York: Capricorn Books.
Dufrenne, Mikel (1973). *Phenomenology of Aesthetic Experience.* Evanston: Northwestern University Press.
Eisenberg, Arnold. (1988) *Aesthetics and Theory of Art Criticism.* Chicago: University of Chicago Press.
Focillon, Henri (1942). *The Life of Forms.* Translated by C. B. Hogan and G. Kubles, New Haven: Yale University Press.
Gaut, Berys and Lopes, Dominic MacIver (2000). *The Routledge Companion to Aesthetics.* New York: Rutledge.
Gaimari, Giulia. (2020) *Ethics, Politics, and Justice in Dante.* Chicago: University of Chicago Press.
Girard, Rene (1961). *Deceit, Desire, and the Novel: Self and Other Literary Structure.* Translated by Yvonne Freccero, Baltimore: John Hopkins Press.
Goldblatt and Lee Brown (2005), *Aesthetics: A Reader in Philosophy of the Arts,* Upper Saddle River: Prentice Hall.
Goldman, Alan H. (2016). *Philosophy and the Novel.* Oxford: Oxford University Press.
Gaarder, Jostein, Paulette Moller. (1994). *Sophie's World: A Novel about the History of Philosophy.* New York: Farrar, Straus, and Giroux.
Gibbons, Reginald. (2015) *How Poems Think.* Chicago: University of Chicago Press.
Hagberg, Gary. (2021). Editor. *Reflection in Fictional World.* London: Palgrave Macmillan, (forthcoming).
Hegel, G.W.F. (1998) *Aesthetics.* Oxford: Oxford University Press.
Hozzette, Valerie. (2015). *Wuthering Heights on Film and Television.* Chicago: Chicago University Press.
Heidegger, Martin (1993). *The Origin of the Work of Art, The Essence of Truth in Martin Heidegger: Basic Writings.* translated by John Sallis and A. Hofstadter. New York: Rutledge.
Heidegger, Martin (2013) *Poetry, Language, and Thought.* Translated by Albert Hofstadter. New York: Harper Perennial Classics.
Herman, D., Jahn, M. and Ryan, M. L. (eds). (2005). *The Routledge Encyclopedia of Narrative Theory.* London: Routledge.
Hesse, Hermann (1968). *Narcissus and Goldmund.* New York: Picador.
Hospers, John (1964). *Meaning and Truth.* Hamden: Archon Books.
Jones, Peter. (1975). *Philosophy and the Novel.* Oxford: Oxford University Press.
Jeffrey, Leo. (2020) *Philosophy as World Literature.* London: Bloomsbury Publishing.

Jeffrey, Leo. (2021) *The Bloomsburg Handbook of World Theory*. London: Bloomsburg Publishing.
Ingarden, Roman. (1973). *The Literary Work of Art, Evanston*. Iniana: Northewestern University Press.
Kierman, Mathew (2006). *Aesthetics and the Philosophy of Art*. Hoboken: Blackwell.
Kreitman, Norman (2020). *The Roots of Metaphor: A Multidisciplinary Study in Aesthetics*. Routledge.
Kuczynska, Alicja (2018). *Art as a Philosophy*, in *Dialogue and Universalism*, issue 28; (1988); "Qualities of Things and Aesthetic qualities," in Mitias (1988), *Aesthetic Quality and Aesthetic Experience*.
Lamarque, Peter and Haugom Stein. (1994). *Truth, Fiction, and Literature*. Oxford: At the Clarendon Press; 2008. *Philosophy of Literature*. Oxford: Blackwell.
Landy, Joshua (2004). *Philosophy as Fiction: Self, Deception, and Knowledge in Proust*. Oxford: Oxford University Press.
Langer, Susan. (1951). *Philosophy in a New Key*. Cambridge: Harvard University Press.
Levinson, Jerrold. (2017) *Aesthetic Pursuits*. Oxford: Oxford University Press.
Livingston, P. (2009). "Narrativity and Knowledge". *Journal of Aesthetics and Art Criticism*, 67 (11): 25–36.
Mahfouz, Naguib (2016) *On Literature and Philosophy*. Chicago: Chicago University Press. 67, pp. 25–36.
McKeon, Zahava. (1982). *Novels and Arguments*. Chicago: University of Chicago Press.
Merleau-Ponty, Maurice. (2005). *The Phenomenology of Perception*. New York: Rutledge Publishing.
Mikken, Jukka (2008). "Philosophical Fiction and the Art of Fiction-Making." *SATS* (2): 116–132.
Mitias, Michael. (1987). *What Makes an Experience Aesthetic?* Rodopi; *The Possibility of Aesthetic Experience*. Amsterdam: *Kluwer, 1987*; *Aesthetic Quality and Aesthetic Experience*. Amsterdam: Rodopi, 1988; *The Philosopher and the Devil*, London: Olympia, 2018.
Nanay, Bence. (2016) *Aesthetics as a Philosophy of Perception*. Oxford: Oxford University Press.
Nyongesa, Andrew. (2018) *Tintinnabulation of Literary Theory*. African Books Collective.
Osborn, Carly. (2021) *Tragic Novels and the American Dream*. London: Bloomsburg Publishing.
Phelan, J. and Rabinowitz, P.J. (eds) (2005). *A Companion to Narrative Theory*. Oxford: Blackwell.
Pinheiro, Marilia. (2015) *Philosophy and the Ancient Novel*. Casemate, UK: Oxbow books

Pippin, Robert. (2021) *Philosophy by Other Means*. Chicago: University of Chicago Press.
Porter, Burton (2004). *Philosophy Through Fiction and Film*. Upper Sadler River: Pearson Prentice-Hall.
Putner, David (2007). *Metaphor*. New York: Routledge.
Reiner, Schumann. (2022) *The Place of the Symbolic*. Chicago: University of Chicago Press.
Reyerson, James (2011). "The Philosophical Novel." New York: *New York Times Sunday Book Review*.
Rousseau, Jean Jacques. (1953). *The Confessions of Jean Jacques Rousseau*. Translated by J. M. Cohen. Baltimore: Penguin.
Smith, Barry (1980). "Ingarden and Meinong on the Logic of Fiction." *Philos. Phenomenological Res.*, 41 (1/2): 93–105.
Schlegel, August W. (2004) *Lectures on Dramatic Art and Literature*. Kessinger Publishing.
Stecker, Barry. (2018). *Philosophy of the Novel*. London: Palgrave Macmillan.
Stolnitz, Jerome. (1992). "On the Cognitive Triviality in Art". British Journal of Aesthetics, vol. 32, pp. 191–200.
Tolstoy, Leo. (2021) *What Is Art?* Compass Circle.
Turco, Lewis. (2020) *The Book of Literary Terms: The Genres of Fiction, Drama, Non-Fiction, and Literary Criticism*. University of New Mexico Press.
Verene, Donald P. (2018). *The Philosophy of Literature*. Eugene: Wipf and Stock.
Weitz, Morris. (1950). *Philosophy of the Arts*. Cambridge: Harvard University Press.
Whittock, Trevor. (1992). "The Role of Metaphor in Dance," *The British Journal of Philosophy*, Vol. 32, Number 3.
Wilson, Katherine. (1983). "Knowledge and Literature", *Philosophy*, vol. 58, pp. 489–96.
Young, James (2001) *Art and Knowledge. London*, Routledge.

Index

A
Aesthetic experience, 5, 9, 12, 13, 15, 16, 20, 23, 25, 26, 28, 31, 34–36, 43, 44, 46, 47, 54, 58–61, 63–65, 69–71, 75–80, 82, 87, 88, 90, 100
Aesthetic object, 5, 7, 15, 16, 25–28, 34, 35, 44, 46, 47, 57–63, 65, 69, 70, 72, 75–82, 88, 100, 116, 119–122, 124, 137
Aesthetic quality, 4–7, 12, 13, 15, 16, 26, 43, 46, 47, 54–56, 60, 62, 63, 66, 69, 71, 75–78, 80, 82, 88, 96, 100, 103, 120
Aristotle, 4, 8, 16, 40, 41, 87, 101–104, 107, 114, 115
Artistic distinction, 6, 26, 54, 69, 76
Artwork, 5–7, 13, 15, 17, 18, 47, 54–56, 58–61, 63, 66, 69–71, 75–82, 87, 88, 92, 128
Aurelius, Marcus, 88

B
Beethoven, Ludwig van, 59

C
Camus, Albert, 1, 131
Cassirer, Ernst, 13
Conrad, Joseph, 77

D
DaVinci, Leonardo, 18, 77, 81, 82
Descartes, Rene, 87
Dostoevsky, Fyodor, 8, 11, 36, 56, 57, 59, 61, 64, 66, 71, 75, 92–96, 100, 107, 117, 121, 122, 131
Duchamp, Marcel, 55

E
Eidetic thinking language, 56
Expression, 2, 3, 17, 33, 43, 47, 56, 58, 61, 65, 66, 74, 83, 84, 89, 91, 92, 100, 102, 128

G
Gogol, Nicolai, 71

H
Hardy, Thomas, 27, 28, 30, 84
Hegel, Georg W.F., 71, 87
Heidegger, Martin, 90, 91
Hesse, Herman, 34, 36, 37, 40–42

I
Ideal, 5, 14, 32, 49, 50, 80, 83, 86, 88, 92, 93, 95, 96, 112, 113, 118, 122, 124–126
Intuition, 2, 18, 33, 34, 63, 71–74, 85, 90–92, 104, 127–130, 137

K
Kant, Immanuel, 87
Knowledge, 1–3, 6–8, 14, 16, 24, 32, 33, 38, 46, 48–53, 58, 64, 69–97, 99–101, 104–108, 115–117, 120, 124–138

L
Literariness, 4, 7, 13–28, 31, 36, 48, 53, 54, 86
Literary distinction
  genre, 27–31
  novel, 13, 27–31, 69, 75, 99

M
Mann, Thomas, 61, 66, 131
Matisse, Henri, 72
Meaning
  realm of, 5, 14, 48, 59, 86, 89, 90, 125
  world of, 5, 7, 11, 12, 18, 20, 21, 23–25, 27, 28, 31, 34, 35, 44, 58–61, 71, 82, 88, 96, 120
Melville, Herman, 1, 61, 66, 71, 131
Michaelangelo, 41, 59

N
Novel
  literary, 1–4, 6–44, 47, 48, 53, 61–64, 66, 70, 73–75, 83–86, 88, 89, 91, 99, 119–121, 137, 138
  philosophical, 1–3, 5–8, 12, 31, 35, 36, 38, 44–66, 69–97, 99, 100, 107, 119–138

P
Philosophicalness, 4, 31–36, 39, 47–53, 62–66, 84, 86, 99, 100, 119–124
Plato, 4, 8, 51, 87, 90, 104–106, 115, 130
Potentiality, 4, 6, 7, 11, 15, 16, 20, 23, 25, 26, 28, 31, 33–35, 44, 46, 51, 54, 56–58, 63, 69–72, 74, 76–78, 80, 81, 91, 100, 108, 121, 122, 126–128
Proust, Marcel, 36, 61, 66, 71, 131

R
Rodin, Auguste, 3, 35
Russel, Bertrand, 88

S
Significant form, 5, 7, 11–13, 15–18, 20–24, 26, 28, 31, 34–36, 43, 54, 55, 57–64, 69–71, 75–80, 82, 88, 120–122, 124
Sophocles, 55, 64
Story, 4, 6, 7, 9–13, 15–17, 20–24, 26, 37, 38, 43, 46, 47, 53, 54, 56, 58, 64, 65, 69, 83, 88, 96, 103, 120–124

T
Thackery, William, 27
Theme, 1, 5–7, 9–12, 14, 21, 23–31, 38, 39, 43–46, 54, 70, 72, 74, 75, 77, 79–81, 84, 85, 99, 107, 121–123, 128, 131
Tolstoy, 1, 8, 10, 11, 20–22, 24, 26, 29, 30, 59, 63, 66, 71, 72, 84, 90, 120, 131, 133, 134, 136–138

U
Unamuno, Miguel de, 90

V
Value, 2, 5–7, 10, 11, 13–15, 17, 24, 25, 29, 32–36, 38, 39, 43, 45, 48–53, 55, 56, 59, 71, 76, 77, 80, 82–84, 86–88, 90–92, 96, 107, 111–118, 121, 123–129, 131, 137
realm of, 49, 51, 86, 90–92, 125, 127
Vermeer, Jan, 55

W
Whitehead, Alfred N., 26, 71, 87, 88, 127